Mastering Modular JavaScript

Nicolás Bevacqua

Beijing · Boston · Farnham · Sebastopol · Tokyo

Mastering Modular JavaScript

by Nicolás Bevacqua

Published by O'Reilly Media, Inc., 1005 Gravenstein Highway North, Sebastopol, CA 95472.

O'Reilly books may be purchased for educational, business, or sales promotional use. Online editions are also available for most titles (*http://oreilly.com/safari*). For more information, contact our corporate/institutional sales department: 800-998-9938 or *corporate@oreilly.com*.

Acquisitions Editor: Allyson MacDonald	**Indexer:** Angela Howard
Editor: Virginia Wilson	**Interior Designer:** Monica Kamsvaag
Production Editor: Colleen Cole	**Cover Designer:** Randy Comer
Copyeditor: Sharon Wilkey	**Illustrator:** Rebecca Demarest
Proofreader: Jasmine Kwityn	

September 2018:   First Edition

Revision History for the First Edition
2018-08-24:   First Release

See *http://oreilly.com/catalog/errata.csp?isbn=9781491955680* for release details.

The O'Reilly logo is a registered trademark of O'Reilly Media, Inc. *Mastering Modular JavaScript*, the cover image, and related trade dress are trademarks of O'Reilly Media, Inc.

The views expressed in this work are those of the author and do not represent the publisher's views. While the publisher and the author have used good faith efforts to ensure that the information and instructions contained in this work are accurate, the publisher and the author disclaim all responsibility for errors or omissions, including without limitation responsibility for damages resulting from the use of or reliance on this work. Use of the information and instructions contained in this work is at your own risk. If any code samples or other technology this work contains or describes is subject to open source licenses or the intellectual property rights of others, it is your responsibility to ensure that your use thereof complies with such licenses and/or rights.

978-1-491-95568-0
[LSI]

Table of Contents

Preface

Long after the printing press was invented, publishing books remains a challenging endeavor. Yes, there's typically an author (or authors) who scribble the content wherever and whenever they find time to do so. But there's also a content editor, tasked with helping the author transform their stream of consciousness into a relatable story that's not too dry to read—something to be especially careful about when it comes to technical or business books. We have the technical reviewers, watchful subject-matter experts on the lookout for egregious mistakes in technical definitions or interpretations. And lastly, of course, we have the copyeditor, the typo linters of prose and last bastion of proper grammar. Thus far, however, we've barely scratched the surface: everyone mentioned here is interested mostly in the contents of the book, but there are other aspects to the bookmaking process as well. There's also, as an example, the typesetter, whose job is to ensure that the book looks good when it goes to print—bidding good riddance to orphans and widows, poorly wrapped lines of code, and so much more. Someone has to design the cover, and another person must approve the table of contents for the first draft so that the author gets a contract. In addition, several people oversee the process that culminates in the book going to press, usually referred to as production. Once copies are printed, they need to be distributed. Eventually, the book hits the shelves (physical or otherwise) and starts selling. Someone buys the book and finally starts to read it. We could write entire books about the purchase transaction alone.

The complexity of the whole process is mind-boggling, and yet, to each individual, it's not that complicated. The author, for example, merely has to write a few hundred words every day. Where did all that complexity go? There's a reason the process is so compartmentalized: we're not that good at handling high-level complexity. Breaking it into single responsibilities (such as "write content," "improve how prose flows," "review technical concerns," "fix grammar mistakes," "typeset for production," or "handle purchases") is what makes the process simpler for individuals working on the mammoth project that is writing a book, or just about any business enterprise.

Publishing is merely an example—we could do this exercise with just about anything. Pick an object on your desk, any object. Think about how it got there. Now zoom out, think some more: How was it made? What is it made of? How many people were involved in manufacturing each piece, assembling it, perfecting it, and getting it to the store where it was bought? Is it a fruit? How many people were involved in planting it, fighting off pests, pruning plants, packaging the fruit, and getting it to the store where it was bought?

Software is not all that different, except complexity is all around us. At the deepest zoom levels, we find constraints defined by physical constants such as the speed of light, individual bits and hardware, interrupt calls, assembly language, and much more. Zooming out, we find the megastructures of the technology sector, which handle everything from search queries to payment processing. Somewhere in the midst of all this complexity, there's us developers and the projects bestowed upon us.

We hardly stop to think about the complexity underlying everyday objects and interactions, since doing so would be paralyzing. Instead, we hide solutions behind abstract interfaces, so much that they *become*—in our minds—the interface. Some of these interfaces map well to the abstracted implementation, and they feel great. Others don't map all that well to the implementation, and we end up feeling confused and frustrated. Software is not at all different. We don't want to think about the system as a whole, and virtually everything we work with sits behind interfaces that are simpler to use and understand than their underlying implementations.

Who Should Read This Book

This book is meant for developers, enthusiasts, and professionals with a working knowledge of JavaScript and ES6.[1] These developers, and anyone interested in learning more about writing modular code that's readable, maintainable, and scalable, even beyond the JavaScript language, shall benefit from reading *Mastering Modular JavaScript*.

Why Modular JavaScript?

I started toying with Node.js—and, unbeknownst to me, getting into a serious relationship with JavaScript—at about the same time that I discovered open source and fell in love with its practices. Coming from the closed-source landscape in C#, the open source ecosystem around Node.js gave me a new perspective and joy in figuring out how to write robust code that others find pleasant enough to consume. It's with this background that I find myself always pondering about how an interface should be defined, who would be consuming it, and how they'd like to spend their time doing something else than figuring out what we originally intended them to do.

The goal of this book is to offer an affable way of becoming a successful module author. It's not that writing JavaScript modules is particularly difficult; however, following sound design practices to ensure that we deliver the right amounts of simplicity and flexibility so that consumers can rely on modules to be simple most of the time (but flexible when it matters) while keeping internal complexity in check—is hardly a trivial task. I wrote bits and pieces about proper application design in *JavaScript Application Design*[2] and for the Pony Foo blog, but I've been yearning to publish something more comprehensive that was exclusively dedicated to reasoning about, designing, and writing modular code.

---

1 ES6 effected a profound change in the JavaScript language, introducing multiple syntax improvements and a few handfuls of new methods. This book assumes familiarity with JavaScript after ES6. You can learn more about ES6 syntax by visiting the Pony Foo blog (*https://mjavascript.com/out/es6*) for a crash course.

2 *JavaScript Application Design* (*https://mjavascript.com/out/jad*) is a book I published through Manning in 2015. It revolves around build processes, but also features chapters on managing complexity, sensible asynchronous flow control code, REST API design, and JavaScript testing concerns.

Though I couldn't find any books that addressed the subject from a JavaScript point of view, you can easily find other books that touch on the subject of modular code, such as *Code Complete* by Steve McConnell (Microsoft Press) or *Clean Code* by Robert C. Martin (Prentice Hall), and leverage their teachings in your JavaScript development efforts. *Mastering Modular JavaScript* is an attempt to draw attention away from what others think you should be doing, and instead enable you to come to your own conclusions about what you should be doing and why—without imposing axiomatic rules that only contribute to what artificially self-proclaims and positions itself as "clean code."

Without being too overt, this book tries to explain how you could be writing modular code. Instead, we'll try to shed light on the fundamentals behind modular architecture, and its history when it comes to JavaScript, so that you have a better understanding of what it means to write modular applications and what's to be gained from doing so.

While there are heaps of books on proper application design, there isn't a lot of material to be found on the topic of modular application design, let alone modular JavaScript application design—hence this book. While the majority of the advice, musings, and teachings in this book aren't at all specific to JavaScript, the fresh focus on JavaScript means you'll be learning about how to write modular web applications while keeping in mind the quirks that make the web such a unique platform and make JavaScript special in many ways.

Rather than rely on long-winded, pages-long, thoroughly analyzed, concrete examples, the book hopes to challenge you to apply its passages to the problems that you're trying to address in your own programs, and coming to your own realizations by weighing the benefits and drawbacks of taking one of a few possible approaches. In software, there is no such thing as one-size-fits-all, and you're often going to leverage your own best judgment to decide how to write it. All software adapts to the context that surrounds it, and if you've done any work at all involving software deployments or releases, then you surely are intimate with exactly how hard it is to cram the same piece of software into different execution environments.

Just as with *Practical Modern JavaScript*, this book has the goal of establishing a baseline, bit by bit. After having learned all about the latest language features in *Practical Modern JavaScript*, we'll use this book to learn all about modular design thinking. This incremental and modular approach is meant to be pervasive in both books, across each chapter, and each section.

How Is This Book Organized?

Chapter 1 discusses the evolution of modularity in the context of JavaScript, from the early days of embedding JavaScript in `onclick` attributes, to CommonJS and finally native ECMAScript modules. It then looks at the benefits of writing self-contained code, and of doing so at every level of a system: services, applications, components, modules, functions, blocks, and so on.

Chapter 2 covers the essentials of modular design, giving you a foundation from which you can write modules that are conscientious of their API surface, how it's (in all likelihood) going to be consumed, where the responsibilities lie, and what belongs on the interface.

A good portion of Chapter 3 is devoted to understanding the kinds of problems you should be solving, and how to do so while keeping an eye on the way the module and its interface may evolve, and being shy about abstractions while waiting for clear patterns to emerge. This chapter prods beneath the surface to get you thinking of best practices around documentation, error handling, and following your own reasoning by applying your own context to the problem that is being resolved.

In Chapter 4, we get comfortable talking about internal complexity, tight coupling, and weighing the merits of frameworks and conventions. The bulk of this chapter is spent discussing some of the many ways in which we can reduce complexity by refactoring our code. We then discuss the role of state in relation to complexity, and how it can be mitigated. Data structures play a role as well, as selecting the right ones is both challenging and immensely rewarding when it comes to keeping complexity in check.

Chapter 5 is specifically about JavaScript, detailing how we can leverage modern language constructs to write clear programs. This chapter also examines patterns such as inheritance and composition, leading into a discussion about which option is better, depending on your use case. The chapter is rounded out by tackling classic patterns like revealing modules, object factories, event emitters, and JSON message passing.

Chapter 6 describes the mindset of a battle-hardened module developer, addressing security concerns and dependency management, build and integration processes, interfaces and abstractions, and generally a potpourri of module design advice and best practices.

Those of you who are already familiar with the history of modularity when it comes to JavaScript would do well to, at the very least, skim through the history lessons in the first chapter. If you're more of the type who's comfortable jumping around the pages in a book, I would still recommend reading through every chapter, given this relatively short book is more of a story to be told about well-reasoned programs than it is a compendium of recipes.

Conventions Used in This Book

The following typographical conventions are used in this book:

Italic
: Indicates new terms, URLs, email addresses, filenames, and file extensions.

`Constant width`
: Used for program listings, as well as within paragraphs to refer to program elements such as variable or function names, databases, data types, environment variables, statements, and keywords.

> This element signifies a general note.

O'Reilly Safari

Safari (formerly Safari Books Online) is a membership-based training and reference platform for enterprise, government, educators, and individuals.

Members have access to thousands of books, training videos, Learning Paths, interactive tutorials, and curated playlists from over 250 publishers, including O'Reilly Media, Harvard Business Review, Prentice Hall Professional, Addison-Wesley Professional, Microsoft Press, Sams, Que, Peachpit Press, Adobe, Focal Press, Cisco Press, John Wiley & Sons, Syngress, Morgan Kaufmann, IBM Redbooks, Packt, Adobe Press, FT Press, Apress, Manning, New Riders, McGraw-Hill, Jones & Bartlett, and Course Technology, among others.

For more information, please visit *http://oreilly.com/safari*.

How to Contact Us

Please address comments and questions concerning this book to the publisher:

O'Reilly Media, Inc.
1005 Gravenstein Highway North
Sebastopol, CA 95472
800-998-9938 (in the United States or Canada)
707-829-0515 (international or local)
707-829-0104 (fax)

We have a web page for this book, where we list errata, examples, and any additional information. You can access this page at *http://bit.ly/mastering-modular-javascript*.

To comment or ask technical questions about this book, send email to *bookquestions@oreilly.com*.

For more information about our books, courses, conferences, and news, see our website at *http://www.oreilly.com*.

Find us on Facebook: *http://facebook.com/oreilly*

Follow us on Twitter: *http://twitter.com/oreillymedia*

Watch us on YouTube: *http://www.youtube.com/oreillymedia*

Acknowledgments

There are a lot of people to thank for *Mastering Modular JavaScript* coming to fruition. First and foremost is Virginia Wilson, the main content editor in charge of this book and the Modular JavaScript series at O'Reilly. She offered insight where it counted, was very understanding when my schedule tightened and the writing slowed to a trickle, and always kept an extremely positive attitude about things!

The technical reviewers were also out of this world. Mathias Bynens focused on making sure my comments around the ECMAScript specification were up to par, as usual. Ingvar Stepanyan always seems ready to jump at the chance to help out with technical reviews for my books, and he's always offering unique points of view that result in clearer descriptions and more thorough examples, I'm incredibly grateful for his work. Adam Rackis has also been super helpful during technical review for the series, always providing solid commentary about bits that needed to be corrected, better fleshed out, or clarified.

I would be remiss if I didn't call out everyone who backed the Indiegogo campaign for the Modular JavaScript book series back in 2016. Thank you for placing your trust in me when these books were merely an idea, injecting me with a large dose of enthusiasm early on. If we ever run into each other, the beers are on me!

In no particular order:

Aaron Endsley, Aaron Hans, Aaron Olson, Aaron Wells, Adam Rackis, Adi Purnama Mutiara, Adrian Li, Adrian Rand, Agustin Nicolas Polo, Alan Chandler, Alasdair Shepherd, Alejandro Nanez, Alexis Mills, Allen Dean, Anastasios Alexiou, Andrea Giammarchi, Andres Mijares, Andrew Broman, Andrew Kenward, Andrew Shell, Andrew Van Slaars, Andrey Golovin, Angel Ramirez Morel, Anna Vu, Anselm Hannemann, Anthony Casson, Arnau Pujol, Arnis Lupiks, Artur Jonczyk, Aziz Khoury, Barney Scott, Beau Cronin, Ben Lagoutte, Ben Mann, Benjamin Bank, benjamintpoon, Benny Neugebauer, Bishal Pantha, Bran Sorem, Brent Huffman, Bruce Hyatt, Burton Podczerwinski, Béla Varga, Ca-Phun Ung, Cameron Stark, Carlos López, Casper de Rooij, Chad Thoreson, Charles Herman, Charles Rector, Charlie Hill, Chase Hagwood, Chris Fothergill, Chris Weber, Christopher Dresel, Christopher Gonzales, Christopher Hamilton, Christopher Scott, Cindy Juarez, Claudia Hernández, Constantin Chirila, Cris Ryan Tan, Dallen Richard Loder, Dan Hayden, Dan M., Dan Perrera, Dan Rocha, Daniel Cloud, Daniel Egger, Daniel Sleeth, David Ershag, David G. Chaves, David González Polán, David Hobbs, David Lemarier, Dayan Barros, Dejan

Cencelj, Denise Darmawi, Derick Rodriguez, Derik Badman, Dick Grayson, Dmitry Goryunov, Don Hamilton III, Donald Gary, Doug Chase, Dumitru Florin Gabriel, Eder Sánchez, Edgar Barrantes, Edouard Baudry, Eduardo Rabelo, Eric Lezotte, Ersan Temizyurek, Ezequiel Cabrera, Fabian Marz, Fabio Vedovelli, Fabrice Le Coz, Federico Foresti, Fer To, Fernando Ripoll Lafuente, Flavio Spaini, Fran Nunez, Francesco Strappini, Francisco Cerdas, Fredrik Forsmo, Fredrik Lexberg, Gabor Dolla, Gabriel Chertok, Gabriel García Seco, Gergo Szonyi, Giovanni Londero, glennjonesnet, Gorshunov Vladimir, Guy Tepper, Hamish Macpherson, Hanslutter Fomben, Henk Jan van Wijk, Hernan Chiosso, Horváth László Gábor, Hugo Lopes, Ian B. De La Cruz, Ian Doyle, Ian McCausland, Ignacio Anaya, Istvan Szmozsanszky, Ivan Saveliev, Ivan Tanev, J. Singh, Jack Pallot, Jack W McNicol, Jaime García, Jake Smith, Janderson Martins, Jani Kraner, Jared Moran, Jason Broyles, Jason Finch, Jean Osorio, Jeffrey Borisch, Jelena Jovanovic, Jennifer Dixon, Jeremy Tymes, Jeremy Wilken, Jia Fei Fei, Jiaxing Wang, Joachim Kliemann, Joan Maria Talarn, Johannes Weiser, John Engstrom, John Fogarty, John Johnson, Jon Saw, Jonathan Boiser, Joostc Schermers, Josh Adam, Josh Magness, José Esparza, jsnisenson, Juan Lopez, Junrou Nishida, Jörn Flath, Karthikeya Pammi, Kevin Gimbel, Kevin Rambaud, Kevin Scheffelmeier, Kevin Youkhana, kgarbaya, konker, Kostas Galanos, Kris Bulman, Kyle Simpson, Lalit Agrawala, Lea P., Leonardo Di Lella, Lidor Lapid, mailtorenil, Marc Grabanski, Marco Martins, marco.scarpa, Marcus Bransbury, Mariano Campo, Mark Kramer, Martijn Rouwendal, Martin Ansty, Martin Gonzalez, Martin Luna, Massimiliano Filacchioni, Mathias Bynens, Matt Riley, Matt Webb, Matteo Hertel, Matthew Bagwell, Mauro Gestoso, Max Felgenhauer, Maxwell Chiareli, Michael Chan, Michael Erdey, Michael Klose, Michael Kühnel, Michael Spreu, Michael Vezzani, Mike Kidder, Mike Parsons, Mitchell Gates, Nathan Heskew, Nathan Schlehlein, Nick Dunn, Nick Klunder, Nicolás Isnardi, Norbert Sienkiewicz, Oliver Wehn, Olivier Camon, Olivier Van Hamme, Owen Densmore, P. Ghinde, Patrick Nouvion, Patrick Thompson, Paul Aeria, Paul Albertson, Paul Cooper, Paul Grock, Paul Kalupnieks, Paul Kamma, Paul Vernon, Paula Penedo Barbosa, Paulo Elias, Per Fröjd, Peter deHaan, Peter Holzer, Peter Piekarczyk, peterdoane, Phan An, Piotr Seefeld, Pranava S Balugari, Rahul Ravikumar, Randy Ferrer, Renato Alonso, Rey Bango, Reynaldo Tortoledo, Ric Johnson, Ricardo Pereira, Richard Davey, Richard Hoffmann, Richard Weltman, Riyadh Al Nur, Robert Buchholz, Ron Male, Ryan

Castner, Ryan Ewing, Rylan Cottrell, Salvatore Torcivia, Sean Esteva, Sebastian Brieschenk, Sergey Efremov, Sergey Melnikov, Shane Eckel, Shaunak Kashyap, Shawn Searcy, Simeon Vincent, simonkeary, Stefan Boehm, Steve Mahony, Steven Kingston, Stoyan Delev, Stuart Robson, Sumit Sarkar, Swizec Teller, Szabolcs Legradi, Tanner Donovan, Ted Young, Thee Sritabtim, Thomas Noe, Thomas Schwarz, Tim Goshinski, Tim Osborn, Tim Pietrusky, Tony Brown, Tudosa Razvan, Ture Gjørup, Umar Farooq Khawaja, Uri Chandler, Victor Rosell, Vinay Puppal, Vladimir Bruno, Vladimir Simonov, Vladimir Zeifman, Wayne Callender, Wayne Patterson, Wee Keat Liew, Wes Bos, Wonmin Jeon, Yann LE CORRE, Yevgen Safronov, Yonatan Mevorach, youbiteme, Zach Gottlieb, Zachary Hawkins, Zane Thomas, 坤福 曾, @agolveo, @amstarri, @bondydaa, @cbergenhem, @cde008, @changke, @dhtrinh02, @dlteron.green, @eduplessis, @eonilsson, @fogarty.tj, @fortune, @gm.schlereth, @illusionmh, @jcnoble2, and @michael!

As usual, I'd also like to thank my wife, Marianela, for always standing right beside me through the emotional roller coaster that is writing these books. I don't know how she does it.

CHAPTER 1

Module Thinking

As discussed in the Preface, complexity seems to be all around us while we're working on software projects. So are abstractions, which keep complexity hidden away from us under rocks we don't dare touch. These rocks are our interfaces to the rest of the world so that we can get away with hardly thinking about it. JavaScript is no exception here. On the contrary, as powerful as dynamic languages are, it is also that much easier, and even tempting, to write complex programs when we're using them.

To get started, let's discuss how we can better apply abstractions, interfaces, and their underlying concepts to the work we do. We then can minimize the amount of complexity we need to stare at when working on a project, a feature, a piece of functionality, down to the branches of a single function.

1.1 Introduction to Module Thinking

Embracing *module thinking* is understanding that complexity is, ultimately, inescapable. At the same time, that complexity can be swept under an interface, hardly to ever be seen or thought of again. But—and here's one of the tricky parts—the interface needs to be well-designed so that its users don't become frustrated. That frustration could even lead us to peering under the hood and finding that the implementation is vastly more complex than the poor interface we're frustrated by, and maybe if the interface didn't exist in the first place, we'd be better off in terms of maintainability and readability.

Systems can be organized granularly: we can split them into projects, made of multiple applications, containing several application-level layers, where we can have hundreds of modules, made up of thousands of functions, and so on. A granular approach helps us write code that's easy to understand and maintain, by attaining a reasonable degree of modularity, while preserving our sanity. In Section 1.4, "Modular Granularity," on page 11, we'll discuss how to best leverage this granularity to create modular applications.

Whenever we delineate a component, there's going to be a public interface that other parts of the system can leverage to access our component. The interface, or API, comprises the set of methods or attributes that our component exposes. These methods or attributes can also be referred to as *touchpoints*—the aspects of the interface that can be publicly interacted with. The fewer touchpoints an interface has, the smaller its surface area, and the simpler the interface becomes. An interface with a large surface area is highly flexible, but might also be a lot harder to understand and use, given the high amount of functionality exposed by the interface.

This interface serves a dual purpose. It allows us to develop new bits and pieces of the component, exposing only functionality that's ready for public consumption while keeping private everything that's not meant to be shared with other components. At the same time, it allows consumers—components or systems that are leveraging our interface—to reap the benefits of the functionality we expose, without concerning themselves with the details of how we implemented that functionality.

Robust, documented interfaces are one of the best ways of isolating a complicated piece of code so that others can consume its functionality without knowing any implementation details. A systematic arrangement of robust interfaces can be accrued to form a layer, such as service or data layers in enterprise applications. In doing so, we might be able to largely isolate and circumscribe logic to one of those layers, while keeping presentational concerns separate from strictly business- or persistence-related concerns. Such a forceful separation is effective because it keeps individual components tidy and layers uniform. Uniform layers, composed of components similar in pattern or shape, offer a sense of familiarity that makes them more straightforward to consume on a sustained basis from the point of view of a single developer, who over time becomes ever more used to familiar API shapes.

Relying on consistent API shapes is a great way of increasing productivity, given the difficulty of coming up with adequate interface designs. When we consistently leverage similar API shapes, we don't have to come up with new designs every time, and consumers can rest assured that you haven't reinvented the wheel every time. We'll discuss API design at length over the coming chapters.

1.2 A Brief History of Modularity

When it comes to JavaScript, modularity is a modern concept. In this section, we'll quickly revisit and summarize the milestones in the evolution of modularity in the world of JavaScript. This section isn't meant to be a comprehensive list, by any means, but instead to illustrate the major paradigm changes along the history of Java-Script.

1.2.1 Script Tags and Closures

In the early days, JavaScript was inlined in HTML `<script>` tags. At best, it was offloaded to dedicated script files, all of which shared a global scope.

Any variables or bindings declared in one of these files or inline scripts would be imprinted on the global `window` object. This created leaks across entirely unrelated scripts that might've led to conflicts or even broken experiences, as a variable in one script might inadvertently replace a global that another script was relying on:

```
<script>
  var initialized = false

  if (!initialized) {
    init()
  }

  function init() {
    initialized = true
    console.log('init')
  }
</script>

<script>
  if (initialized) {
```

```
  console.log('was initialized!')
}

// even `init` has been implicitly made a global variable
console.log('init' in window)
</script>
```

Eventually, as web applications started growing in size and complexity, the concept of scoping and the dangers of a global scope became evident and more well-known. Immediately Invoked Function Expressions (IIFE) were invented and became an instant mainstay. An IIFE worked by wrapping an entire file or portions of a file in a function that executed immediately after evaluation. Each function in JavaScript creates a new level of scoping, meaning var variable bindings would be contained by the IIFE. Even though variable declarations are hoisted to the top of their containing scope, they'd never become implicit globals, thanks to the IIFE wrapper, thus suppressing the brittleness of implicit JavaScript globals.

Several flavors of IIFE can be found in the next example snippet. The code in each IIFE is isolated and can escape onto the global context only via explicit statements such as window.fromIIFE = true:

```
(function() {
  console.log('IIFE using parenthesis')
})()

~function() {
  console.log('IIFE using a bitwise operator')
}()

void function() {
  console.log('IIFE using the void operator')
}()
```

Using the IIFE pattern, libraries would typically create modules by exposing and then reusing a single binding on the window object, thus minimizing global namespace pollution. The next snippet shows how we might create a mathlib component with a sum method in one of these IIFE-based libraries. If we wanted to add more modules to mathlib, we could place each of them in a separate IIFE that adds its own methods to the mathlib public interface, while anything else could stay private to the component that defined the new portion of functionality:

```
void function() {
  window.mathlib = window.mathlib || {}
  window.mathlib.sum = sum

  function sum(...values) {
    return values.reduce((a, b) => a + b, 0)
  }
}()

mathlib.sum(1, 2, 3)
// <- 6
```

This pattern was, coincidentally, an open invitation for JavaScript tooling to burgeon, allowing developers to—for the first time—concatenate every IIFE module into a single file. This reduced the strain on the network, provided the primitive bundling solutions that existed at the time were able to figure out their way around automatic semicolon insertion and minified content without breaking your application logic.

The problem with the IIFE approach was that there wasn't an explicit dependency tree. Developers had to manufacture component file lists in a precise order so that dependencies would load before any modules that depended on them did—recursively.

1.2.2 RequireJS, AngularJS, and Dependency Injection

This is a problem we've hardly had to think about ever since the advent of module systems like RequireJS or the dependency injection mechanism in AngularJS, both of which allowed us to explicitly name the dependencies of each module.

The following example shows how we might define the *mathlib/ sum.js* library using RequireJS's define function, which was added to the global scope. The returned value from the define callback is then used as the public interface for our module:

```
define(function() {
  return sum

  function sum(...values) {
    return values.reduce((a, b) => a + b, 0)
  }
})
```

We could then have a *mathlib.js* module that aggregates all functionality we wanted to include in our library. In our case, the dependency is just *mathlib/sum*, but we could list as many as we wanted in the same way. We'd list each dependency by using their paths in an array, and we'd get their public interfaces as parameters passed into our callback, in the same order:

```
define(['mathlib/sum'], function(sum) {
  return { sum }
})
```

Now that we've defined a library, we can consume it by using `require`. Notice how the dependency chain is resolved for us in this snippet:

```
require(['mathlib'], function(mathlib) {
  mathlib.sum(1, 2, 3)
  // <- 6
})
```

This is the upside in RequireJS and its inherent dependency tree. Regardless of whether our application contains a hundred or thousands of modules, RequireJS resolves the dependency tree without needing a carefully maintained list. Given that we've listed dependencies exactly where they are needed, we've eliminated the necessity for a long list of every component and their relationships to one another, as well as the error-prone process of maintaining such a list. Eliminating such a large source of complexity is merely a side effect, but not the main benefit.

This explicitness in dependency declaration, at a module level, made it obvious how a component was related to other parts of the application. That explicitness, in turn, fostered a greater degree of modularity, something that was ineffective before because of how hard it was to follow dependency chains.

RequireJS wasn't without problems. The entire pattern revolved around its ability to asynchronously load modules, which was ill-advised for production deployments because of how poorly it performed. Using the asynchronous loading mechanism, you issued hundreds of network requests in a waterfall fashion before much of your code was executed. A different tool would have to be used to optimize builds for production. Then there was the verbosity factor; you'd end up with long lists of dependencies, a RequireJS function call, and the callback for your module. On that note, there were quite a few RequireJS functions and several ways of invoking those functions, complicating its use. The API wasn't the most intuitive, because there were so many ways of doing the same thing: declaring a module with dependencies.

The dependency injection system in AngularJS suffered from many of the same problems. It was an elegant solution at the time, relying on clever string parsing to avoid the dependency array, using function parameter names to resolve dependencies instead. This mechanism was incompatible with minifiers, which would rename parameters to single characters and thus break the injector.

Later in the lifetime of AngularJS v1, a build task was introduced that would transform code like the following:

```
module.factory('calculator', function(mathlib) {
  // ...
})
```

into the format of the following bit of code, which was minification-safe because it included the explicit dependency list:

```
module.factory('calculator', ['mathlib', function(mathlib) {
  // ...
}])
```

Needless to say, the delay in introducing this little-known build tool, combined with the overengineered aspect of having an extra build step to un-break something that shouldn't have been broken, discouraged the use of a pattern that carried such a negligible benefit anyway. Developers mostly chose to stick with the familiar RequireJS-like hardcoded dependency array format.

1.2.3 Node.js and the Advent of CommonJS

Among the many innovations hailed by Node.js, one was the CommonJS module system, or CJS for short. Taking advantage of the fact that Node.js programs had access to the filesystem, the CommonJS standard is more in line with traditional module-loading mechanisms. In CommonJS, each file is a module with its own scope and context. Dependencies are loaded using a synchronous `require` function that can be dynamically invoked at any time in the lifecycle of a module, as illustrated in this snippet:

```
const mathlib = require('./mathlib')
```

Much like RequireJS and AngularJS, CommonJS dependencies are also referred to by a pathname. The main difference is that the boilerplate function and dependency array are now both gone, and the interface from a module could be assigned to a variable binding, or used anywhere a JavaScript expression could be used.

Unlike RequireJS or AngularJS, CommonJS was rather strict. In RequireJS and AngularJS, you could have many dynamically defined modules per file, whereas CommonJS had a one-to-one mapping between files and modules. At the same time, RequireJS had several ways of declaring a module, and AngularJS had several kinds of factories, services, providers, and so on—besides the fact that its dependency injection mechanism was tightly coupled to the AngularJS framework itself. CommonJS, in contrast, had a single way of declaring modules. Any JavaScript file was a module, calling `require` would load dependencies, and anything assigned to `module.exports` was its interface. This enabled better tooling and code introspection, making it easier for tools to learn the hierarchy of a CommonJS component system.

Eventually, Browserify was invented as a way of bridging the gap between CommonJS modules for Node.js servers and the browser. Using the `browserify` command-line interface program and providing it with the path to an entry-point module, one could combine an unthinkable number of modules into a single browser-ready bundle. The killer feature of CommonJS, the npm package registry, was decisive in aiding its takeover of the module-loading ecosystem.

Granted, npm wasn't limited to CommonJS modules or even JavaScript packages, but that was and still is by and large its primary use case. The prospect of having thousands of packages (now over half a million and steadily growing) available in your web application at the press of a few fingertips, combined with the ability to reuse large portions of a system on both the Node.js web server and each client's web browser, was too much of a competitive advantage for the other systems to keep up.

1.2.4 ES6, import, Babel, and Webpack

With ES6 becoming standardized in June 2015, and Babel transpiling ES6 into ES5 long before then, a new revolution was quickly approaching. The ES6 specification included a module syntax native to JavaScript, often referred to as ECMAScript modules (ESM).

ESM is largely influenced by CJS and its predecessors, offering a static declarative API as well as a promise-based dynamic programmable API, as illustrated here:

```
import mathlib from './mathlib'
import('./mathlib').then(mathlib => {
  // ...
})
```

In ESM, too, every file is a module with its own scope and context. One major advantage in ESM over CJS is how ESM has—and encourages—a way of statically importing dependencies. Static imports vastly improve the introspection capabilities of module systems, given they can be analyzed statically and lexically extracted from the abstract syntax tree (AST) of each module in the system. Static imports in ESM are constrained to the topmost level of a module, further simplifying parsing and introspection. Another advantage of ESM over CommonJS require() is that ESM specifies a way of doing asynchronous module loading, which implies that parts of an application's dependency graph could be loaded in response to specific events, concurrently, or lazily as needed. Although this feature is not yet implemented in most environments at the time of this writing, there is strong indication that Node.js would incorporate it in the future.[1]

In Node.js v8.5.0, ESM support was introduced behind an --experimental-modules flag, provided that we use the *.mjs* file extension for our modules. Most evergreen browsers already support ESM without flags.

Webpack is a successor to Browserify that largely took over the role of universal module bundler, thanks to a broader set of features. Just as in the case of Babel and ES6, Webpack has long supported ESM with both its static import and export statements as well as the dynamic import() function-like expression. It has made a particularly fruitful adoption of ESM, in no little part thanks to the introduction of a "code-splitting" mechanism, whereby it's able to partition an application into different bundles to improve performance on first-load experiences.[2]

---

1 You can dive into the specifics by reading "The Current State of Implementation and Planning for ESModules" (*https://mjavascript.com/out/esm-node*) by a member of the Node.js team, Myles Borins.

2 Code splitting (*https://mjavascript.com/out/code-splitting*) lets you split your application into several bundles based on different entry points, and also lets you extract dependencies shared across bundles into a single reusable bundle.

Given how ESM is native to the language (as opposed to CJS), it can be expected to completely overtake the module ecosystem in a few years.

1.3 The Perks of Modular Design

We've already addressed the fact that modularity, as opposed to a single shared global scope, helps avoid unexpected clashes in variable names thanks to the diversification of scoping across modules. Beyond a fix for clashes, modularity spread across files limits the amount of complexity we have to pay attention to when working on any one particular feature. As a result, our team is able to focus on the task at hand and be more productive.

Maintainability, or the ability to effect change in the codebase, also improves significantly because of this. When code is simple and modular, it's easier to build upon and extend. Maintainability is valuable regardless of team size: even in a team of one, if we leave a piece of code untouched for a few months and then come back to it, it might be hard to improve upon or even understand if we didn't consider writing maintainable code the first time around.

Modular code is meant to be highly maintainable by default. By keeping pieces of code simple and following the single responsibility principle (SRP), whereby each aims to fulfill only one goal, and combining these simple pieces of code into more-sophisticated components, we're able to compose our way to larger components, and eventually to an entire application. When each piece of code in a program is modular, the codebase appears to be simple when we're looking at individual components, yet on the whole, it is able to exhibit complex behaviors, just like the book-publishing process we discussed at the beginning of this chapter.

Components in modular applications are defined by their interfaces. The implementation of those components is not their essence, but their interfaces are. When interfaces are well-designed, they can be grown in nonbreaking ways, augmenting the number of use cases they can satisfy, without compromising existing usage. When we have a mindfully designed interface, the implementation behind that interface becomes easy to tweak or swap entirely. Strong interfaces are effective at hiding away weak implementations, which can be later refactored into more robust implementations, provided the interface holds. Strong interfaces are also excellent for unit testing because we won't have to worry about the implementation and can test the interface—the inputs and outputs of a component or function. If the interface is well tested and robust, we can surely consider its implementation in a secondary plane.

Given that those implementations are secondary to the foremost requirement of having intuitive interfaces, which aren't coupled to their implementations, we can concern ourselves with the trade-off between flexibility and simplicity. Flexibility inevitably comes at the cost of added complexity, which is a good reason not to offer flexible interfaces. At the same time, flexibility is often a necessity, and thus we need to strike the right balance by deciding how much rigidity we can get away with in our interfaces. This balance would mean an interface appeases its consumers thanks to its ease of use, but that it also enables advanced or more uncommon use cases when needed, without too much of a detrimental effect on the ease of use or at the cost of greatly enhanced implementation complexity.

We'll discuss the trade-offs between flexibility, simplicity, composability, and the right amount of future-proofing in the following couple of chapters.

1.4 Modular Granularity

We can apply modular design concepts on every level of a given system. If a project's demands outgrow its initial scope, maybe we should consider splitting that project into several, smaller projects with smaller teams that are more manageable. The same can be said of applications: when they become large or complex enough, we might want to split them into differentiated products.

When we want to make an application more maintainable, we should consider creating explicitly defined layers of code so that we can grow each layer horizontally while preventing the complexity of those additions from spreading to other, unrelated, layers. The same thought process can be applied to individual components, splitting them into two or more smaller components that are then tied together by yet another small component, which could act as a composition layer whose sole responsibility is knitting together several underlying components.

At the module level, we should strive to keep functions simple and expressive, with descriptive names and not too many responsibilities. Maybe we'll have a function dedicated exclusively to pulling together a group of tasks under a particular asynchronous flow, while having other functions for each task that we need to perform within that control flow. The topmost flow-controlling function could be exposed as a public interface method for our module, but the only part of it that should be treated as a public interface are the parameters that we receive as inputs for that function and the output produced by that same topmost function. Everything else becomes an implementation detail and is, as such, to be considered swappable.

The internal functions of a module won't have as rigid of an interface either: as long as the public interface holds, we can change the implementation—including the interfaces of functions that make up that implementation—however we want. This is not to say, however, that we should treat those interfaces any less deliberately. The key to proper modular design is in having the utmost respect for all interfaces, and that includes the interfaces exposed by internal functions.

Within functions, we also need to componentize aspects of the implementation, giving those aspects a name in the way of function calls, deferring complexity that doesn't need to be immediately dealt with in the main body of the function until later in the read-through of a given piece of code. We're writing programs that are meant to be readable and writable for other humans and even ourselves in the future. Virtually everyone who has done any amount of programming has experienced a feeling of frustration when glancing at a piece of code they themselves wrote a few months prior, only to later realize that, with a fresh pair of eyes, the design they had then come up with wasn't as solid as they originally intended.

Remember, computer program development is largely a human and collaborative endeavor. We're not optimizing for computers to run programs as fast as possible. If we were, we'd be writing binary or hardcoding logic into circuit boards. Instead, our focus is to empower an organization so that its developers can remain productive and quickly understand and even modify pieces of code they haven't run across before. Working under the soft embrace of conventions and practices, which place developers on an even keel, closes that cycle by making sure future development is consistent with the way the application has taken shape up until the present.

Going back to performance, we should be treating it as a feature, and for the most part we shouldn't place a higher premium on it than we would for other features. Unless performance needs to be a defining feature of our system for business reasons, we shouldn't worry about ensuring that the system runs at top speed on all code paths. Doing so is bound to result in highly complex applications that are hard to maintain, debug, extend, and justify.

We, as developers, often overdo architecture as well, and a lot of the reasoning about performance optimization applies here. Laying out an all-encompassing architecture that has the potential to save us trouble as we scale to billions of transactions per second might cost us considerable time spent up front and possibly also lock us into a series of abstractions that will be hard to keep up with, for no foreseeable gains in the near term. It's a lot better when we focus on problems we're already running into, or might soon run into, instead of trying to plan for a hockey-stick growth of infrastructure and throughput without any data to back up the hockey-stick growth we're anticipating.

When we don't plan in such a long-term form, an interesting thing occurs: our systems grow more naturally, adapting to the needs of the near-term, gradually progressing toward support for a larger application and larger set of requirements. When that progression is gradual, we notice a corrective behavior in the way abstractions are picked up or discarded as we grow. If we settle on abstractions too early, and they end up being the wrong abstractions, we pay dearly for that mistake. Bad abstractions force us to bend entire applications to their will. After we've realized that the abstraction is bad and ought to be removed, we might be so heavily invested in it that pulling out might be costly. This, paired with the sunk cost fallacy, whereby we're tempted to keep the abstraction just because we've spent a lot of time, sweat, and blood on it, can be hazardous indeed.

We'll devote an important part of this book to understanding how to identify and leverage the right abstractions at the right time so that the risk we incur is minimized.

1.5 Modular JavaScript: A Necessity

Because of its history, JavaScript is particularly interesting when it comes to modular design. In the early days of the web, and for a long time, no established practices existed, and few people knew the language beyond showing alert boxes. As a highly dynamic language that wasn't yet mature enough, JavaScript was at an odd place between statically typed languages like Java or C#, and more heavily used dynamic languages like Python or PHP.

The lack of native modularity on the web—due to the way a program is loaded in chunks using HTML <script> tags—is in stark contrast to any other execution environments, where programs can be made up of any number of files and modular architectures are natively supported by the language, its compiler, and its filesystem-based environment. On the web, we're only now barely beginning to scratch the surface of native modules, something other programming environments have had since their inception. As discussed in Section 1.2, "A Brief History of Modularity," on page 3, the lack of a native module-loading mechanism, paired with the lack of native modules beyond just files that shared a global scope, forced the web community to get creative in its approach to modularity.

The native JavaScript modules specification that eventually landed in the language was heavily influenced by this community-led effort. Even as of this writing, we're still probably two or three years away from being able to use the native module system effectively on the web. Patterns that have been adopted universally elsewhere, like layered or component-based architectures, haven't even been contemplated on the web for most of its lifetime thus far.

Until the launch of a Gmail beta client in April 2004, which demonstrated the power of asynchronous JavaScript HTTP requests to provide a single-page application experience, and then the initial release of jQuery in 2006, which provided a hassle-free cross-browser web development experience, JavaScript was seldom regarded as a serious modern development platform.

With the advent of frameworks like Backbone.js, AngularJS, Ember.js, and React, new techniques and breakthroughs also made an uptick on the web:

- Writing code under ES6 and beyond, but then transpiling parts of that code down to ES5 to attain broader browser support
- Shared rendering, using the same code on both server and client to render a page quickly on initial page load and continue to load pages quickly upon navigation

- Automated code bundling, packing the modules that an application comprises into a single bundle for optimized delivery

- Bundle-splitting along routes so that there are several bundles outputted, each optimized for the initially visited route; CSS bundling at the JavaScript module level so that CSS (which doesn't feature a native module syntax) can also be split across bundles

- Myriad ways of optimizing assets such as images at compile time, improving productivity during development while keeping production deployments highly performant

These are all part of the iterative nature of innovation in the web.

This explosion of innovation doesn't stem from sheer creativity alone but also from necessity: web applications are getting increasingly complex, as is their scope, purpose, and requirements. It follows logically, then, that the ecosystem around them would grow to accommodate those expanded requirements, in terms of better tooling, better libraries, better coding practices, architectures, standards, patterns, and more choice in general.

In the next chapter, we'll break down the meaning of *complexity*, and start building fortifications against complexity in the programs we write. By following a few rules for encapsulating logic across layers upon layers of components, we'll commence our journey to simpler program design.

CHAPTER 2

Modularity Principles

Modularity can be the answer to complexity, but what exactly do we mean when we're talking about complexity?

Complexity is a loaded term for a nuanced topic. What does *complex* mean? A dictionary defines complex as something that's "composed of many interconnected parts" but that's not the problem we generally refer to when we speak of complexity in the context of programming. A program may have hundreds or thousands of files and still be considered relatively simple.[1]

The next two definitions, offered by that same dictionary, might be more revealing in the context of program design.

- "Characterized by a very complicated or involved arrangement of parts, units, etc."
- "So complicated or intricate as to be hard to understand or deal with"

The first definition indicates that a program can become complex when its parts are arranged in a complicated manner; the interconnections among parts become a pain point. This could stem from convoluted interfaces or a lack of documentation, and it's one of the aspects of complexity that we'll tackle in this book.

---

1 Further details of the dictionary definition (*https://mjavascript.com/out/complex*) might help shed light on this topic.

We can interpret the second definition as the other side of the complexity coin. Components can be so complicated that their implementation is hard to understand, debug, or extend. Most of the book is devoted to counterbalancing and avoiding this aspect of complexity.

In broad terms, something is complex when it becomes hard to grasp or fully understand. By that definition, anything in a typical program can be complex: a block of code, a single statement, the API layer, its documentation, tests, the directory structure, coding conventions, or even a variable's name.

Measuring complexity by lines of code proves to be trite: a file with thousands of lines of code can be simple if it's just a list of constants like country codes or action types. Conversely, a file with two dozen lines of code could be insurmountably complex, not only in its interface but particularly in its implementation. Add together a few complex components and soon you'll want nothing to do with the codebase.

Cyclomatic complexity is the number of unique code paths a program can take, and it may be a better metric when measuring the complexity of a component. Cyclomatic complexity allows us to measure only how complex a component has become. On its own, however, tracking this metric does little to significantly reduce complexity across our codebase or improve our coding style.

We must acknowledge that codebases are not fixed in time. Codebases typically grow along with time, much like the products we build with them. There is no such thing as a finished product or the perfect codebase. We should develop application architecture that embraces the passage of time through the ability to adjust to new conditions.

A significant body of changes to an implementation should be able to leave the API in front of that implementation unmodified. It should be possible to extend the API surface of a component with ease, and ironing out the wrinkles of an outdated API shouldn't be fraught with confusion or frustration. When we want to horizontally scale our program beyond single components, it should be straightforward instead of having to modify several existing components in order to accommodate each new one. How can modular design help us manage complexity both at the component level and at scale?

2.1 Modular Design Essentials

Modularity tackles the complexity problem in program design by opting for small modules with a clear-cut and well-tested API that's also documented. Defining a precise API attacks interconnection complexity, while small modules aim to make programs easier to understand and work with.

2.1.1 Single Responsibility Principle

The single responsibility principle (SRP) is perhaps the most widely agreed upon principle of successful modular application design. Components are said to follow SRP when they have a single, narrow objective.

Modules that follow SRP do not necessarily have to export a single function as their API. As long as the methods and properties we export from a component are related, we aren't breaking SRP.

When thinking in terms of SRP, it's important to figure out what the responsibility is. Consider, as an example, a component used to send emails through the Simple Mail Transfer Protocol (SMTP). The choice to send emails using SMTP could be considered an implementation detail. If we later want the ability to render the HTML to be sent in those emails by using a template and a model, would that also pertain to the email-sending responsibility?

Imagine we developed email sending and templating in the same component. These would be tightly coupled. Furthermore, if we later wanted to switch from SMTP to the solution offered through the API for a transactional email provider, we'd have to be careful not to interfere with the templating capability that lies in the same module.

The following code snippet represents a tightly coupled piece of code that mixes templating, sanitization, email API client instantiation, and email sending:

```
import insane from 'insane'
import mailApi from 'mail-api'
import { mailApiSecret } from './secrets'
function sanitize (template, ...expressions) {
  return template.reduce((result, part, i) =>
    result + insane(expressions[i - 1]) + part
  )
}
```

```
export default function send (options, done) {
  const {
    to,
    subject,
    model: { title, body, tags }
  } = options
  const html = sanitize`
    <h1>${ title }</h1>
    <div>${ body }</div>
    <div>
    ${
      tags
        .map(tag => `${ <span>${ tag }</span> }`)
        .join(` `)
    }
    </div>
    `
  const client = mailApi({ mailApiSecret })
  client.send({
    from: `hello@mjavascript.com`,
    to,
    subject,
    html
  }, done)
}
```

It might be better to create a separate component that's in charge of rendering HTML based on a template and a model, instead of adding templating directly in the email-sending component. We could then add a dependency on the email module so that we can send that HTML, or we could create a third module where we're concerned only with the wiring.

Provided its consumer-facing interface remained the same, an independent SMTP email component would be interchangeable with a component that sent emails some other way, such as via an API, logging to a data store, or writing to standard output. In this scenario, the way in which emails are sent would be an implementation detail, while the interface becomes more rigid as it's adopted by more modules. An inflexible interface gives us flexibility in the way the task is performed, while allowing implementations to be replaced with ease according to the use case at hand.

The following example shows an email component that's concerned only with configuring the API client and adhering to a thoughtful interface that receives the to recipient, the email subject, and its html body, and then sends the email. This component has the sole purpose of sending email:

```
import mailApi from 'mail-api'
import { mailApiSecret } from './secrets'

export default function send(options, done) {
  const { to, subject, html } = options
  const client = mailApi({ mailApiSecret })
  client.send({
    from: `hello@mjavascript.com`,
    to,
    subject,
    html
  }, done)
}
```

It wouldn't be hard to create a drop-in replacement by developing a module that adheres to the same send API but sends email in a different way. The following example uses a different mechanism, whereby we simply log to the console. Even though it doesn't actually send any emails, this component could be useful for debugging purposes:

```
export default function send(options, done) {
  const { to, subject, html } = options
  console.log(`
    Sending email.
    To: ${ to }
    Subject: ${ subject }
    ${ html }`
  )
  done()
}
```

By the same token, a templating component could be developed orthogonally, with an implementation that's not directly tied into email sending. The following example is extracted from our original coupled implementation, but is concerned only with producing a piece of sanitized HTML by using a template and the user-provided model:

```
import insane from 'insane'

function sanitize(template, ...expressions) {
  return template.reduce((result, part, i) =>
    result + insane(expressions[i - 1]) + part
  )
}
```

```
export default function compile(model) {
  const { title, body, tags } = model
  const html = sanitize`
    <h1>${ title }</h1>
    <div>${ body }</div>
    <div>
    ${
      tags
        .map(tag => `${ <span>${ tag }</span> }`)
        .join(` `)
    }
    </div>
    `

  return html
}
```

Slightly modifying the API shouldn't be an issue, as long as it remains consistent across the components we want to make interchangeable. For instance, a different implementation could take a template identifier, in addition to the model object, so that the template itself is also decoupled from the compile function.

When we keep the API consistent across implementations,[2] using the same signature across every module, it's easy to swap out implementations depending on context such as the execution environment (development versus staging versus production) or any other dynamic context that we need to rely upon.

As mentioned earlier, a third module could plumb together different components that handle separate concerns, such as templating and email sending. The following example leverages the logging email provider and the static templating function to join both concerns together. Interestingly, this module doesn't break SRP either, as its only concern is to plumb other modules together:

```
import { send } from './email/log-provider'
import { compile } from './templating/static'

export default function send (options, done) {
  const { to, subject, model } = options
  const html = compile(model)
  send({ to, subject, html }, done)
}
```

---

2 For example, one implementation might merely compile an HTML email by using inline templates, another might use HTML template files, another could rely on a third-party service, and yet another could compile emails as plain-text instead.

We've been discussing API design in terms of responsibility, but something equally interesting is that we've hardly worried about the implementation of those interfaces. Is there merit to designing an interface before digging into its implementation?

2.1.2 API First

A module is only as good as its public interface. A poor implementation may hide behind an excellent interface. More important, a great interface means we can swap out a poor implementation as soon as we find time to introduce a better one. Since the API remains the same, we can decide whether to replace the existing implementation altogether or whether both should coexist while we upgrade consumers to use the newer one.

A flawed API is a lot harder to repair. Several implementations may follow the interface we intend to modify, meaning that we'd have to change the API calls in each consumer whenever we want to make changes to the API itself. The number of API calls that potentially have to adapt increases with time, entrenching the API as the project grows.

Having a mindful design focus on public interfaces is paramount to developing maintainable component systems. Well-designed interfaces can stand the test of time by introducing new implementations that conform to that same interface. A properly designed interface should make it simple to access the most basic or common use cases for the component, while being flexible enough to support other use cases as they arise.

An interface often doesn't have the necessity of supporting multiple implementations, but we must nonetheless think in terms of the public API first. Abstracting the implementation is only a small part of the puzzle. The answer to API design lies in figuring out which properties and methods consumers will need, while keeping the interface as small as possible.

When we need to implement a new component, a good rule of thumb is drawing up the API calls we'd need to make against that new component. For instance, we might want a component to interact with the Elasticsearch REST API. Elasticsearch is a database engine with advanced search and analytics capabilities, and its documents are stored in indices and arranged by type.

In the following piece of code, we're fantasizing with an `./elastic search` component that has a public `createClient` binding, which returns an object with a `client#get` method that returns a `Promise`. Note how detailed the query is, making up what could be a real-world keyword search for blog articles tagged `modularity` and `java script`:

```
import { createClient } from './elasticsearch'
import { elasticsearchHost } from './secrets'

const client = createClient({
  host: elasticsearchHost
})
client
  .get({
    index: `blog`,
    type: `articles`,
    body: {
      query: {
        match: {
          tags: [`modularity`, `javascript`]
        }
      }
    }
  })
  .then(response => {
    // ...
  })
```

Using the `createClient` method, we could create a client, establishing a connection to an Elasticsearch server. If the connection is dropped, the component we're envisioning will seamlessly reconnect to the server, but on the consumer side, we don't necessarily want to worry about that.

Configuration options passed to `createClient` might tweak how aggressively the client attempts to reconnect. A `backoff` setting could toggle whether an exponential back-off mechanism should be used: the client waits for increasing periods of time if it's unable to establish a connection.

An `optimistic` setting that's enabled by default could prevent queries from settling in rejection when a server connection isn't established, by having them wait until a connection is established before they can be made.

Even though the only setting explicitly outlined in our imagined API usage example is `host`, it would be simple for the implementation to support new settings in its API without breaking backward compatibility.

The `client#get` method returns a promise that'll settle with the results of asking Elasticsearch about the provided `index`, `type`, and query. When the query results in an HTTP error or an Elasticsearch error, the promise is rejected. To construct the endpoint, we use the `index`, `type`, and the `host` that the `client` was created with. For the request payload, we use the `body` field, which follows the Elasticsearch Query DSL.[3] Adding more `client` methods, such as `put` and `delete`, would be trivial.

Following an API-first methodology is crucial in understanding how the API might be used. By placing our foremost focus on the interface, we are purposely avoiding the implementation until there's a clear idea of what interface the component should have. Then, once we have a desired interface in mind, we can begin implementing the component. Always write code against an interface.

Note how the focus is not only on what the example at hand addresses directly but also on what it doesn't address: room for improvement, corner cases, how the API might change going forward, and whether the existing API can accommodate more uses without breaking backward compatibility.

2.1.3 Revealing Pattern

When everything in a component is made public, nothing can be considered an implementation detail, and thus making changes becomes hard. Prefixing properties with an underscore is not enough for consumers not to rely on them; a better approach is not to reveal private properties in the first place.

By exposing only what's meant to be used by external consumers, a component avoids a world of trouble. Consumers don't need to worry about undocumented touchpoints meant for internal use, however tempting, because they're not exposed in the first place. Component makers don't need to be concerned about consumers

---

3 You can check out the Elasticsearch Query DSL documentation (*https://mjava script.com/out/es-dsl*).

using touchpoints that were meant to be internal when they want to internalize them.

Consider the following piece of code, which externalizes the entire implementation of a simple `counter` object. Even though it's not meant to be part of the public API, as indicated by its underscore prefix, the `_state` property is still exposed:

```
const counter = {
  _state: 0,
  increment() { counter._state++ },
  decrement() { counter._state-- },
  read() { return counter._state }
}
export default counter
```

It's better to explicitly expose the methods and properties we want to make public:

```
const counter = {
  _state: 0,
  increment() { counter._state++ },
  decrement() { counter._state-- },
  read() { return counter._state }
}
const { increment, decrement, read } = counter
const api = { increment, decrement, read }
export default api
```

This is akin to the way some libraries were written in the days before JavaScript had proper modules: we would wrap everything in a closure so that it wouldn't leak globals and our implementation would stay private and then return a public API. For reference, the next code snippet shows an equivalent component using a closure instead:

```
(function(){
  const counter = {
    _state: 0,
    increment() { counter._state++ },
    decrement() { counter._state-- },
    read() { return counter._state }
  }
  const { increment, decrement, read } = counter
  const api = { increment, decrement, read }
  return api
})()
```

When exposing touchpoints on an interface, it's important to gauge whether consumers need the touchpoint at all, how it helps them, and whether it could be made simpler. For instance, instead of exposing several touchpoints the user can select from, the user might be better off with a single touchpoint that leverages the appropriate code path based on provided inputs. At the same time, the component would couple a smaller part of its implementation to its interface.

Thinking in API-first terms can help: if we have a decent idea of the kind of API surface we want, we can then decide how we want to allow consumers to interact with the component.

As new use cases arise and our component system grows, we should stick to an API-first mindset and the revealing pattern, so that the component doesn't suddenly become more complex. Gradually introducing complexity can help us design the right interface for our component. This interface doesn't offer every solution imaginable, but also elegantly solves the consumer's use cases, provided they fall within the responsibility of our component.

2.1.4 Finding the Right Abstractions

Open source software components often get feature requests that are overly specific to the needs of one particular user. Taking feature requests or requirements at face value is not enough. Instead, we need to dive deeper and find commonalities between the feature that's being requested, features that we may have planned for our roadmap, and features we might want to adapt our component to support in the future.

Granted, it's important for a component to satisfy the needs of most of its consumers, but this doesn't mean we should attempt to satisfy use cases one by one, or in isolation. Almost invariably, doing so results in duplicated logic, inconsistency at the API level, and several ways of accomplishing the same goal, often with inconsistent observed results.

When a commonality can be found, abstractions involve less friction and help avoid the inconsistencies named earlier. Consider, for example, the case of DOM event listeners: we have an HTML attribute and matching JavaScript DOM element property for each event handler, such as onclick, onchange, oninput, and so on. Each property can be assigned a listener function that handles the event. Then there's EventTarget#addEventListener, which has a signature like addEventListener(type, listener, options),[4] centralizing all event-handling logic in a single method that takes the type of event as a parameter. Naturally, this API is better for several reasons. First off, EventTarget#addEventListener is a method, making its behavior clearly defined. Meanwhile, on* handlers are set through assignment, which isn't as clearly defined: when does the effect of assigning an event handler begin? How is the handler removed? Are we limited to a single event handler, or is there a way around it? Are we going to get an error when we assign a nonfunction value as an event listener? Will the raised event result in an error when trying to invoke the nonfunction? Furthermore, new event types can be added transparently to addEventListener, without having to change the API surface, whereas with the on* technique, we would have to introduce yet another property.

Another case in which abstractions come in handy might occur whenever we are dealing with quirks in cross-browser DOM manipulation. It would be superior to have a function like on(element, eventType, eventListener) rather than testing whether addEventListener is supported and deciding which of the various event-listening options is optimal for each case, every time. The abstraction drastically reduces code duplication while also handling every case consistently, limiting complexity.

The preceding cases are clear-cut examples of when an abstraction greatly improves poor interfaces, but that's not always the end result. Abstractions can be a costly way of merging use cases when it's unclear whether those are naturally related in the first place. If we merge use cases too early, we might find that the complexity we're tucking away in an abstraction is quite small—and thus offset by the abstraction's own complexity. If we merge cases that aren't all that related to begin with, we effectively increase complexity and end up creating a tighter coupling than needed. Instead of lowering complexity as we set out to achieve, we end up obtaining the opposite result.

---

4 The options parameter is an optional configuration object that's relatively new to the web API. We can set flags such as capture, which has the same behavior as passing a useCapture flag; passive, which suppresses calls to event.preventDefault() in the listener; and once, which indicates that the event listener should be removed after being invoked for the first time.

It is best to wait until a distinguishable pattern emerges and it becomes clear that introducing an abstraction will help diminish complexity. When such a pattern emerges, we can be confident that the use cases are indeed related, and we'll have better information about whether an abstraction would simplify our code.

Abstractions can generate complexity by introducing new layers of indirection, chipping away at our ability to follow the different code flows around a program. On the other hand, state generates complexity by dynamically modifying the flow in our programs. Without state, programs would run in the same way from start to finish.

2.1.5 State Management

Applications wouldn't do much of anything if we didn't keep state. We need to keep track of things like user input or the page we're currently on to determine what to display and how to help the user. In this sense, state is a function of user input: as the user interacts with our application, state grows and mutates.

Application state comes from stores such as a persistent database or an API server's memory cache. This kind of state can be affected by user interaction, such as when a user decides to write a comment.

Besides state for an individual user and application-wide state, there's also the intermediate state that lies in our program's code. This state is transient and is typically bound to a particular transaction: a server-side web request, a client-side browser tab, and—at a lower level—a class instance, a function call, or an object's property.

We shall think of state as our program's internal entropy. When state reigns, entropy reigns, and the application becomes unbearably hard to debug. One of the goals in modular design is to keep state to the smallest minimum possible. As an application grows larger, so does its state, and the possible state permutations grow with it. Modularity takes aim at this issue by chopping a state tree into manageable bits and pieces; each branch of the tree deals with a particular subset of the state. This approach enables us to contain the growing application state as our codebase grows in size.

A function is deemed *pure* when its output depends solely on its input. Pure functions do not produce any side effects other than the output that's returned. In the following example, the sum function receives a list of numbers and returns the sum of adding all of them together. It is a pure function because it doesn't take into account any external state, and it doesn't emit any side effects:

```
function sum(numbers) {
  return numbers.reduce((a, b) => a + b, 0)
}
```

Sometimes we have a requirement to keep state across function calls. For instance, a simple incremental counter might lead us to implement a module such as the following. The increment function isn't pure, given that count is an external state:

```
let count = 0
const increment = () => count++
export default increment
```

An artifact of this module exporting an impure function is that the outcome of invoking increment hinges upon understanding how it is used elsewhere in the application, as each call to increment changes its expected output. As the amount of code in our program increases, so do the potential ways for an impure function like incre ment to behave, making impure functions increasingly undesirable.

One potential solution is to expose a factory that is itself pure, even when the objects returned by the factory aren't pure. In this piece of code, we're now returning a factory of counters; factory isn't affected by external outputs and is thus considered pure:

```
const factory = () => {
  let count = 0
  const increment = () => count++
  return increment
}
export default factory
```

As long as we limit the usage of each counter spewed by factory to given portions of the application which know about each other's usage, the state becomes more manageable, as we end up with fewer moving parts involved. When we eliminate impurity in public interfaces, we're effectively circumscribing entropy to the calling code. The consumer receives a brand-new counter every time, and it's entirely responsible for managing its state. It can still pass the counter down to its dependents, but it's in control of the way dependents get to manipulate that state, if at all.

This is something we observe in the wild, with popular libraries such as the `request` package in Node.js, which can be used to make HTTP requests.[5] The `request` function relies largely on sensible defaults for the `options` you can pass to it. Sometimes we want to make requests using a different set of defaults.

The library might've offered a solution enabling us to change the default values for every call to `request`. This would've been poor design, as it'd make their handling of `options` more unstable; we'd have to take into account every corner of our codebase before we could be confident about the `options` we'd ultimately end up with when calling `request`.

`request` chose a solution that uses a `request.defaults(options)` method to return an API identical to that of `request`, but with the new defaults applied on top of the existing defaults. This approach avoids surprises, since usage of the modified `request` is constrained to the calling code and its dependents.

2.2 CRUST: Consistent, Resilient, Unambiguous, Simple, and Tiny

A well-regarded API typically packs several of the following traits. It is *consistent*, meaning it is idempotent[6] and has a similar signature shape as that of related functions. It is *resilient*, meaning its interface is flexible and accepts input expressed in a few ways, including optional parameters and overloading. Yet, it is *unambiguous*: there aren't multiple interpretations of how the API should be used, what it does, how to provide inputs, or how to understand the output. Through all of this, it manages to stay *simple*: it's straightforward to use and handles common use cases with little to no configuration, while allowing customization for advanced use cases. Lastly, a CRUST interface is also *tiny*: it meets its goals but isn't overdesigned, it comprises the smallest possible surface area while allowing for future nonbreaking extensibility. CRUST mostly pertains to the outer layer of a system (be it a package, a file, or a function), but its

---

5 You can find `request` on GitHub (*https://mjavascript.com/out/request*).

6 For a given set of inputs, an idempotent function always produces the same output.

principles will seep into the innards of its components and result in simpler code overall.

That's a lot to take in. Let's try to break down the CRUST principle. In this section, we explore these traits, detailing what they mean and why it's important that our interfaces follow them.

2.2.1 Consistency

Humans excel at identifying patterns, and we do so while reading as well. That's partly the reason—besides context—that we can read sentences even when most of the vowels are removed. Deliberately establishing consistent patterns makes our code easier to read, and eliminates surprises requiring us to investigate why two equivalent pieces of code look the same, even though they perform the same job. Could it be that the task they perform is slightly different, or is it just the code that's different, but the end result is the same?

When a set of functions has the same API shape, consumers can intuitively deduce how the next function is used. Consider the native `Array`, where `#forEach`, `#map`, `#filter`, `#find`, `#some`, and `#every` all accept a callback as their first parameter and optionally take the context when calling that callback as their second parameter. Further, the callback receives the current `item`, that item's `index`, and the `array` itself as parameters. The `#reduce` and `#reduceRight` methods are a little different, however, because the callback receives an `accumulator` parameter in the first position, but then it goes on to receive the current `item`, that item's `index`, and the `array`, making the shape quite similar to what we are accustomed to.

As a result, we rarely need to reach for documentation in order to understand how these functions are shaped. The difference lies solely in how the consumer-provided callback is used, and what the return value for the method is. `#forEach` doesn't return a value. `#map` returns the result of each invocation. `#filter` returns only the items for which the callback returns a truthy value. `#some` returns `false` unless the callback returns a truthy value for one of the items, in which case it returns `true` and breaks out of the loop. `#every` returns `false` unless the callback returns a truthy value for every item, in which case it returns `true`.

When we have different shapes for functions that perform similar tasks, we need to make an effort to remember each individual function's shape instead of being able to focus on the task at hand. Consistency is valuable on every level of a codebase: consistent code style reduces friction among developers and conflicts when merging code, consistent shapes optimize readability and give way to intuition, consistent naming and architecture reduces surprises and keeps code uniform.

Uniformity is desirable for any given layer in an application because a uniform layer can be largely treated as a single, atomic portion of the codebase. If a layer isn't uniform, then the consumer struggles to consume or feed data into that part of the application in a consistent manner.

The other side of this coin is resiliency.

2.2.2 Resiliency

Offering interfaces which are consistent with each other in terms of their shapes is important, and making those interfaces accept input in different ways is often just as important, although flexibility is not always the right call. Resiliency is about identifying the kinds of inputs that we should accept, and enforcing an interface where those are the only inputs we accept.

One prominent example of flexible inputs can be found in the jQuery library. With over ten polymorphic overloads[7] on its main $ function, jQuery is able to handle virtually any parameters we throw at it. What follows is a complete list of overloads for the $ function, which is the main export of the jQuery library.

- `$()`
- `$(selector)`
- `$(selector, context)`
- `$(element)`

---

7 When a function has overloaded signatures which can handle two or more types (such as an array or an object) in the same position, the parameter is said to be polymorphic. Polymorphic parameters make functions harder for compilers to optimize, resulting in slower code execution. When this polymorphism is in a hot path—that is, a function that gets called very often—the performance implications have a larger negative impact. Read more about the compiler implications in "What's Up with Monomorphism" (*https://mjavascript.com/out/polymorphism*) by Vyacheslav Egorov.

- `$(elementArray)`
- `$(object)`
- `$(selection)`
- `$(html)`
- `$(html, ownerDocument)`
- `$(html, attributes)`
- `$(callback)`

Though it's common for JavaScript libraries to offer a getter and a setter as overloads of the same method, API methods should generally have a single, well-defined responsibility. Most of the time, this translates into clean-cut API design. In the case of the dollar function, we have three use cases:

- `$(callback)` binds a function to be executed when the DOM has finished loading.
- `$(html)` overloads create elements out of the provided `html`.
- Every other overload matches elements in the DOM against the provided input.

While we might consider selectors and element creation to play the role of getters and setters, the `$(callback)` overload feels out of place. We need to take a step back and realize that jQuery is a decades-old library that revolutionized frontend development due to, in no small part, its ease of use. Back in the day, the requirement to wait for the DOM-ready event was in heavy demand, and so letting consumers listen for the DOM-ready event with the dollar function made sense. Needless to say, jQuery is a unique case, but it's nevertheless an excellent example of how providing multiple overloads can result in a dead-simple interface, even when there are more overloads than users can keep in the back of their heads. Most methods in jQuery offer several ways for consumers to present inputs without altering the responsibilities of those methods.

A new library with a shape similar to jQuery would be a rare find. Modern JavaScript libraries and applications favor a more modular approach, and so the DOM-ready callback would be its own function, and probably its own package. There's still insight to be gained by analyzing jQuery, though. This library has a great user experience because the jQuery interface rarely misinterprets inputs nor produces surprising output. One of the choices observed in jQuery's architecture was not to throw errors that resulted from bugs, user errors in our own code, or invalid selectors, in order to avoid frustrated users. Whenever jQuery finds an inappropriate input parameter, it prefers to return an empty list of matches instead. Silent failures can, however, be tricky: they might leave the consumer without any cues about the problem—whether it's an issue in their code, a bug in the library they're using, or something else.

Even when a library is as flexible as jQuery, it's important to identify invalid input early. As an example, the next snippet shows how jQuery throws an error on selectors it can't parse:

```
$('{div}')
// <- Uncaught Error: unrecognized expression: {div}
```

Besides overloading, jQuery also comes with a wealth of optional parameters. Although overloads are meant as different ways of accepting one particular input, optional parameters serve a different purpose, one of augmenting a function to support more use cases.

A good example of optional parameters is the native DOM `fetch` API. In the next snippet, we have two `fetch` calls. The first one receives only a string for the HTTP resource we want to fetch, and a `GET` method is assumed. In the second example, we've specified the second parameter, and indicated that we want to use the `DELETE` HTTP verb:

```
await fetch('/api/users')
await fetch('/api/users/rob', {
  method: 'DELETE'
})
```

Suppose that, as the API designers for `fetch`, we originally devised it as just a way of doing `GET ${ resource }`. When we get a requirement for a way of choosing the HTTP verb, we could avoid the options object and reach directly for a `fetch(resource, verb)` overload. Although this would serve our particular requirement, it would be shortsighted. As soon as we get a requirement to configure something else, we'd be left with the need to support both `fetch(resource, verb)` and `fetch(resource, options)` overloads, so that we avoid breaking backward compatibility. Worse still, we might be tempted to introduce a third parameter that configures our next requirement. Soon, we'd end up with an API such as the infamous `KeyboardEvent#initKeyEvent` method, whose signature is outlined here:[8]

```
event.initKeyEvent(type, bubbles, cancelable, viewArg,
                   ctrlKeyArg, altKeyArg, shiftKeyArg,
                   metaKeyArg, keyCodeArg, charCodeArg)
```

To avoid this trap, it is paramount to identify the core use case for a function—say, parsing Markdown—and then allow ourselves only one or two important parameters before going for an `options` object. In the case of `initKeyEvent`, the only parameter that we should consider important is the `type`, and everything else can be placed in an `options` object:

```
event.initKeyEvent(type, { bubbles, cancelable, viewArg,
                   ctrlKeyArg, altKeyArg, shiftKeyArg,
                   metaKeyArg, keyCodeArg, charCodeArg })
```

A key aspect of API design is readability. How far can users get without having to reach for the documentation? In the case of `init KeyEvent`, not very; unless they memorize the position of each of 10 parameters and their default values, chances are they're going to reach for the documentation every time. When designing an interface that might otherwise end up with four or more parameters, an `options` object carries a multitude of benefits:

- Consumers can declare options in any order, as the arguments are no longer positional inside the `options` object.
- The API can offer default values for each option. This helps the consumer avoid specifying defaults just so that they can change another positional parameter.[9]
- Consumers don't need to concern themselves with options they don't need.

---

8 See the MDN documentation (*https://mjavascript.com/out/initkeyevent*).

9 Assuming we have a `createButton(size = 'normal', type = 'primary', color = 'red')` method and we want to change its color, we'd have to use `createButton('nor mal', 'primary', 'blue')` to accomplish that, only because the API doesn't have an options object. If the API ever changes its defaults, we'd have to change any function calls accordingly as well.

- Developers reading pieces of code that consume the API can immediately understand which parameters are being used, because they're explicitly named in the options object.

As we make progress, we naturally keep coming back to the `options` object in API design.

2.2.3 Unambiguity

The output shape for a function shouldn't depend on how it received its input or the result that was produced. This rule is almost universally agreed upon: you should aim to surprise consumers of your API as little as possible. In a couple of cases, we may slip up and end up with an ambiguous API. For the same kind of result, we should return the same kind of output.

For instance, `Array#find` always returns `undefined` when it doesn't find any items that match the provided predicate function. If it instead returned `null` when the array is empty, for example, that'd be inconsistent with other use cases, and thus wrong. We'd be making consumers unsure about whether they should test for `undefined` or `null`, and they might end up being tempted to use a loose equality comparison because of that uncertainty, given `== null` matches both `null` and `undefined`.

In the same vein, we should avoid optional input parameters that transform the result into a different data type. Favor composability —or a new method—instead, where possible. An option that indicates whether a raw object such as a `Date` or a DOM element should be wrapped in an instance of jQuery or similar libraries such as `moment` before returning the result, or a `json` option that causes the result to be a JSON-formatted string when `true` and an object otherwise is ill-advised, unless there are technical reasons we must do so.

It isn't necessary to treat failure and success with the same response shape, meaning that failure results can always be `null` or `undefined`, while success results might be an array list. However, consistency should be required across all failure cases and across all success cases, respectively.

Having consistent data types mitigates surprises and improves the confidence a consumer has in our API.

2.2.4 Simplicity

Note how simple it is to use `fetch` in the simplest case: it receives the resource we want to GET and returns a promise that settles with the result of fetching that resource:

```
const res = await fetch('/api/users/john')
console.log(res.statusCode)
// <- 200
```

If we want to take things a bit further, we can chain a `.json()` call onto the response object to find out more about the exact response:

```
const res = await fetch('/api/users/john')
const data = res.json()
console.log(data.name)
// <- 'John Doe'
```

If we instead want to remove the user, we need to provide the `method` option:

```
await fetch('/api/users/john', {
  method: `DELETE`
})
```

The `fetch` function can't do much without a specified resource, which is why this parameter is required and not part of an options object. Having sensible defaults for every other parameter is a key component of keeping the `fetch` interface simple. The `method` defaults to GET, which is the most common HTTP verb and thus the one we're most likely to use. Good defaults are conservative, and good options are additive. The `fetch` function doesn't transmit any cookies by default (a conservative default) but a `credentials` option set to `include` makes cookies work (an additive option).

In another example, we could implement a Markdown compiler function with a default option that supports autolinking resource locators, which can be disabled by the consumer with an `autolinking: false` option. In this case, the implicit default would be `autolinking: true`. Negated option names such as `avoidAuto linking` are sometimes justified because they make it so that the default value is `false`, which on the surface sounds correct for options that aren't user-provided. Negated options, however, tend to confuse users who are confronted with the double negative in `avoidAutolinking: false`. It's best to use additive or positive options, preventing the double negative: `autolinking: true`.

Going back to `fetch`, note how little configuration or implementation-specific knowledge we need for the simplest case. This hardly changes when we need to choose the HTTP verb, since we just need to add an option. Well-designed interfaces make it appear effortless for consumers to use the API for its simplest use case, and have them spend a little more effort for slightly more complicated use cases. As the use case becomes more complicated, so does the way in which the interface needs to be bent. This is because we're taking the interface to the limit, but it goes to show how much work can be put into keeping an interface simple by optimizing for common use cases.

2.2.5 Tiny Surface Areas

Any interface benefits from being its smallest possible self. A small surface area means fewer test cases that could fail, fewer bugs that may arise, fewer ways in which consumers might abuse the interface, less documentation, and more ease of use since there's less to choose from.

The malleability of an interface depends on the way it is consumed. Functions and variables that are private to a module are depended upon only by other parts of that module, and are thus highly malleable. The bits that make up the public API of a module are not as malleable since we might need to change the way each dependent uses our module. If those bits make up the public API of the package, then we're looking at bumping our library's version so that we can safely break its public API without major and unexpected repercussions.

Not all changes are breaking changes, however. We might learn from an interface like the one in `fetch`, for example, which remains highly malleable even in the face of change. Even though the interface is tiny for its simplest use case (`GET /resource`) the `options` parameter can grow by leaps and bounds without causing trouble for consumers, while extending the capabilities of `fetch`.

We can avoid creating interfaces that contain several slightly different solutions for similar problems by holistically designing the interface to solve the underlying common denominator, maximizing the reusability of a component's internals in the process.

Having established a few fundamentals of module thinking and interface design principles, it's time for us to shift our attention to module internals and implementation concerns.

CHAPTER 3

Module Design

Thinking in terms of API-driven and documentation-driven design will yield more usable modules than not doing so. You might argue that internals are not that important: "as long as the interface holds, we can put anything we want in the mix!" A usable interface is only one side of the equation; it will do little to keep the maintainability of your applications in check. Properly designed module internals help keep our code readable and its intent clear. In this chapter, we'll debate about what it takes to write modules with scalability in mind but without getting too far ahead of our current requirements. We'll discuss the CRUST constraints in more depth, and finally elaborate on how to prune modules as they become larger and more complex over time.

3.1 Growing a Module

Small, single-purpose functions are the lifeblood of clean module design. Purpose-built functions scale well because they introduce little organizational complexity into the module they belong to, even when that module grows to 500 lines of code. Small functions are not necessarily less powerful than large functions, but their power lies in composition.

Suppose that instead of implementing a single function with 100 lines of code, we break it up into three or more smaller functions. We might later be able to reuse one of those smaller functions somewhere else in our module, or it might prove a useful addition to its public interface.

In this chapter, we'll discuss design considerations aimed at reducing complexity at the module level. While most of the concerns we'll discuss here have an effect on the way we write functions, it is in the next chapter where we'll be specifically devoting our time to the development of simple functions.

3.1.1 Composability and Scalability

Cleanly composed functions are at the heart of effective module design. Functions are the fundamental unit of our code. We could get away with writing the smallest possible number of functions required, the ones that are invoked by consumers or need to be passed for other interfaces to consume, but that wouldn't get us much in the way of maintainability.

We could rely solely on intuition to decide what deserves to be its own function and what is better left inlined as part of a larger body of code, but this might leave us with inconsistencies that depend on our frame of mind, as well as how each member of a team perceives functions are to be sliced. As we'll see in the next chapter, pairing a few rules of thumb with our own intuition is an effective way of keeping functions simple, limiting their scope.

At the module level, it's required that we implement features with the API surface in mind. When we plan out new functionality, we have to consider whether the abstraction is right for our consumers, how it might evolve and scale over time, and how narrowly or broadly it can support the use cases of its consumers.

When considering whether the abstraction is right, suppose we have a function that's a `draggable` object factory for DOM elements. Draggable objects can be moved around and then dropped in a container, but consumers often have to impose different limitations on the conditions under which the object can be moved, some of which are outlined in the following list:

- Draggable elements must have a parent with a `draggable-list` class.
- Draggable elements mustn't have a `draggable-frozen` class.
- Dragging must initiate from a child with a `drag-handle` class.
- Elements may be dropped into containers with a `draggable-dropzone` class.

- Elements may be dropped into containers with at most six children.

- Elements may not be dropped into the container they're being dragged from.

- Elements must be sortable in the container they're dragged from, but they can't be dropped into other containers.

We've now spent quite a bit of time thinking about use cases for a drag-and-drop library, so we're well equipped to come up with an API that will satisfy most or maybe even every one of these use cases, without dramatically broadening our API surface.

Consider, in contrast, the situation if we were to go off and implement a way of checking off each use case in isolation without taking into account similar use cases, or cases that might arise but are not an immediate need. We would end up with seven ways of introducing specific restrictions on how elements are dragged and dropped. Since we've designed their interfaces in isolation, each of these solutions is likely to be at least slightly different from the rest. Maybe they're similar enough that each of them is an option flag, but consumers still can't help but wonder why we have seven flags for such similar use cases, and they can't shake the feeling that we've designed the interface poorly. But there wasn't much in the way of design; we've mostly tacked requirement upon requirement onto our API surface as each came along, never daring to look at the road ahead and envision how the API might evolve in the future. If we had designed the interfaces with scalability in mind, we might've grouped many similar use cases under the same feature, and would've avoided an unnecessarily large API surface in the process.

Now let's go back to the case where we do spend some time thinking ahead and create a collection of similar requirements and use cases. We should be able to find a common denominator that's suitable for most use cases. We'll know when we have the right abstraction because it'll cater to every requirement we have, and a few we didn't even have to fulfill but that the abstraction satisfies anyhow. In the case of draggable elements, once we've taken all the requirements into account, we might choose to define a few options that impose restrictions based on a few CSS selectors. Alternatively, we might introduce a callback whereby the user can determine whether an element can be dragged and another whereby they can determine whether the element can be dropped. These choices also depend on how heavily the API is going to be used, how flexible we want it to be, and how frequently we intend to make changes to it.

Sometimes we won't have the opportunity to think ahead. We might not be able to foresee all possible use cases. Our forecasts may fail us, or requirements may change, pulling the rug from under our feet. Granted, this never is the ideal situation to find ourselves in, but we certainly wouldn't be better off if we hadn't paid attention to the use cases for our module in aggregate. On the other hand, extra requirements may fit within the bounds of an abstracted solution, provided the new use case is similar enough to what we expected when designing the abstraction.

Abstractions aren't free, but they can shield portions of code from complexity. Naturally, we could boldly claim that an elegant interface such as `fn => fn()` solves all problems in computing; the consumer needs to provide only the right `fn` callback. The reality is, we wouldn't be doing anything but offloading the problem onto the consumers, at the cost of implementing the right solution themselves while still consuming our API in the process.

When we're weighing whether to offer an interface like CSS selectors or callbacks, we're deciding how much we want to abstract, and how much we want to leave up to the consumer. When we choose to let the user provide CSS selectors, we keep the interface short, but the use cases will be limited as well. Consumers won't be able, for example, to decide dynamically whether the element is draggable, beyond what a CSS selector can offer. When we choose to let users provide callbacks, we make it harder for them to use our interface, since they now have to provide bits and pieces of the implementation themselves. However, that expense buys them great flexibility in deciding what is draggable and what is not.

Like most things in program design, API design is a constant trade-off between simplicity and flexibility. For each particular case, it is our responsibility to decide how flexible we want the interface to be, but at the expense of simplicity. We can also decide how simple we want an interface to be, but at the expense of flexibility. Going back to jQuery, it's interesting to note how it always favors simplicity, by allowing you to provide as little information as needed for most of its API methods. Meanwhile, it avoids sacrificing flexibility by offering countless overloads for each of its API methods. The complexity lies in its implementation, balancing arguments by figuring out whether they're a `NodeList`, a DOM element, an array, a function, a selector, or something else (not to mention optional parameters) before even starting to fulfill the consumer's goal when making an API call. Consumers observe some of the complexity at the seams when sifting through documentation and finding out about all the ways of accomplishing the same goals. And yet, despite all of jQuery's internal complexity, code that consumes the jQuery API manages to stay ravishingly simple.

3.1.2 Design for Today

Before we go off and start pondering the best ways of abstracting a feature that we need to implement so that it caters to every single requirement that might come in the future, it's necessary to take a step back and consider simpler alternatives. A simple implementation means we pay smaller up-front costs, but it doesn't necessarily mean that new requirements will result in breaking changes.

Interfaces don't need to cater to every conceivable use case from the outset. As we've analyzed in Chapter 2, sometimes we may get away with first implementing a solution for the simplest or most common use case, and then adding an options parameter through which newer use cases can be configured. As we get to more-advanced use cases, we can make decisions as outlined in the previous section, choosing which use cases deserve to be grouped under an abstraction and which are too narrow for an abstraction to be worthwhile.

Similarly, the interface could start off supporting only one way of receiving its inputs, and as use cases evolve, we might bake polymorphism into the mix, accepting multiple input types in the same parameter position. Grandiose thinking may lead us to believe that, in order to be great, our interfaces must be able to handle every input type and be highly configurable with dozens of configuration options. This might well be true for the most advanced users of our interface, but if we don't take the time to let the interface evolve and mature as needed, we might code our interface into a corner that can then be repaired only by writing a different component from the ground up with a better thought-out interface, and later replacing references to the old component with the new one.

A larger interface is rarely better than a smaller interface that accomplishes the job consumers need it to fulfill. Elegance is of the essence here: if we want our interface to remain small but predict that consumers will eventually need to hook into different pieces of our component's internal behavior so that they can react accordingly, we're better off waiting until this requirement materializes than building a solution for a problem we don't yet have.

Not only will we be focusing development hours on functionality that's needed today, but we'll also avoid creating complexity that can be dispensed with for the time being. It might be argued that the ability to react to internal events of a library won't introduce a lot of complexity. Imagine, however, that the requirement never materializes. We'd have burdened our component with increased complexity to satisfy functionality we never needed. Worse yet, say the requirement changes between the moment we've implemented a solution and the time it's actually needed. We'd now have functionality we never needed, which clashes with different functionality that we do need.

Suppose we don't need hooks only to react to events, but we need those hooks to be able to transform internal state. How would the event hooks' interface change? Chances are, someone might've found a use for the event listeners we implemented earlier, and so we cannot dispose of them with ease. We might be forced to change the event listener API to support internal state transformations, which would result in a cringe-worthy interface that's bound to frustrate implementors and consumers alike.

Falling into the trap of implementing features that consumers don't yet need might be easy at first, but it'll cost us dearly in terms of complexity, maintainability, and wasted developer hours. The best code is no code at all. This means fewer bugs, less time spent writing code, less time writing documentation, and less time fielding support requests. Latch onto that mentality and strive to keep functionality to exactly the absolute minimum that's required.

3.1.3 Abstractions Evolve in Small Steps

It's important to note that abstractions should evolve naturally, rather than have them force an implementation style upon us. When we're unsure about whether to bundle a few use cases with an abstraction, the best option is often to wait and see whether more use cases would fall into the abstraction we're considering. If we wait, and the abstraction holds true for more and more use cases, we can go ahead and implement the abstraction. If the abstraction doesn't hold, we can be thankful we won't have to bend the abstraction to fit the new use cases, often breaking the abstraction or causing more grief than the abstraction had originally set out to avoid on our behalf.

In a similar fashion to that of the preceding section, we should first wait until use cases emerge and then reconsider an abstraction when its benefits become clear. While developing unneeded functionality is little more than a waste of time, leveraging the wrong abstractions will kill or, at best, cripple our component's interface. Although good abstractions are a powerful tool that can reduce the complexity and volume of code we write, subjecting consumers to inappropriate abstractions might increase the amount of code they need to write and will forcibly increase complexity by having users bend to the will of the abstraction, causing frustration and eventual abandonment of the poorly abstracted component.

HTTP libraries are a great example of how the right abstraction for an interface depends entirely on the use cases its consumer has in mind. Plain GET calls can be serviced with callbacks or promises, but streaming requires an event-driven interface that allows the consumer to act as soon as the stream has portions of data ready for consumption. A typical GET request could be serviced by an event-driven interface as well, allowing the implementor to abstract every use case under an event-driven model. To the consumer, this model would feel a bit convoluted for the simplest case, however. Even when we've grouped every use case under a convenient abstraction, the consumer shouldn't have to settle for get('/cats').on('data', gotCats) when their use case doesn't involve streaming. They could be using a simpler get('/cats', gotCats) interface instead, which wouldn't need to handle error events separately, either, instead relying on the Node.js convention whereby the first argument passed to callbacks is an error or null when everything goes smoothly.

An HTTP library that's primarily focused on streaming might go for the event-driven model in all cases because convenience methods such as a callback-based interface could be implemented on top of this minimal interface. This is acceptable; we're focusing on the use case at hand and keeping our API surface as small as possible, while still allowing our library to be wrapped for higher-level consumption. If our library was primarily focused on the experience of leveraging its interface, we might go for the callback- or promise-based approach. When that library then has to support streaming, it might incorporate an event-driven interface. At this point, we'd have to decide whether to expose that kind of interface solely for streaming purposes, or whether it'd be available for commonplace scenarios as well. On the one hand, exposing it solely for the streaming use case keeps the API surface small. On the other, exposing it for every use case results in a more flexible and consistent API, which might be what consumers expect.

Context is of the utmost relevance here. When we're developing an interface for an open source or otherwise broadly available library, we might need to listen to a variety of folks who'll be weighing in on how the API should be designed. Depending on our audience, they may prefer a smaller API surface or a flexible interface. Over time, broadly available libraries tend to favor flexibility over simplicity as the number of users grows, and with them, the number of use cases the library needs to support. When the component is being developed in the context of our day jobs, we might not need to cater to a broad audience. It may well be that we ourselves are the only ones who will be consuming the API, or maybe our team. It might be that we belong to a UI platform team that serves the entire company, which would put us in a situation akin to the open source case, though.

In any case, when we're uncertain whether our interface will be needing to expose certain surface areas, it's highly recommended that we don't expose any of it until we are indeed certain. Keeping API surfaces as small as possible reduces the odds of presenting the consumer with multiple ways of accomplishing the same task. This is often undesirable given that users will undoubtedly become confused and come knocking to ask which one is the best solution. There are a few answers. When the best solution is always the same, the other offerings probably don't belong in our public interface. When the best solution depends on the use case, we should be on the lookout for better abstractions that encapsulate those similar use cases under a single solution. If the use cases are different enough, so should the solutions offered by the interface be, in which case consumers shouldn't be faced with uncertainty: our interface would offer only a single solution for that particular use case.

3.1.4 Move Deliberately and Experiment

You might have heard the "Move Fast and Break Things" mantra from Facebook. It's dangerous to take this mantra literally in terms of software development, which shouldn't be hurried nor frequently broken, let alone on purpose. The mantra is meant to be interpreted as an invitation to experiment; the things we should be breaking are assumptions about how an application architecture should be laid out, how users behave, what advertisers want, and any other assumptions. Moving fast means to quickly hash out prototypes to test our new-found assumptions, to timely seize upon new markets, to avoid engineering slowing to a crawl as teams and requirements grow in size and complexity, and to constantly iterate on our products or codebases.

Taken literally, moving fast and breaking things is a dreadful way to go about software development. Any organization worth its salt would never encourage engineers to write code faster at the expense of product quality. Code should exist mostly because it has to, in order for the products it makes up to exist. The less complex the code we write, provided the product remains the same, the better.

The code that makes up a product should be covered by tests, minimizing the risk of bugs making their way to production. When we take "Move Fast and Break Things" literally, we are tempted to think testing is optional, since it slows us down and we need to move fast. A product that's not covered by tests will be, ironically, unable to move fast when bugs inevitably arise and wind down engineering speed.

A better mantra might be one that can be taken literally, such as "Move Deliberately and Experiment." This mantra carries the same sentiment as the Facebook mantra, but its true meaning isn't meant to be decoded or interpreted. Experimentation is a key aspect of software design and development. We should constantly try out and validate new ideas, verifying whether they pose better solutions than the status quo. We could interpret "Move Fast and Break Things" as

"A/B test early and A/B test often," and "Move Deliberately and Experiment" can convey this meaning as well.[1]

To move deliberately is to move with cause. Engineering tempo will rarely be guided by the development team's desire to move faster, but is most often instead bound by release cycles and the complexity of requirements needed to meet those releases. Of course, everyone wants engineering to move fast where possible, but interface design shouldn't be hurried, regardless of whether the interface we're dealing with is an architecture, a layer, a component, or a function. Internals aren't as crucial to get right, for as long as the interface holds, the internals can be later improved for performance or readability gains. This is not to advocate sloppily developed internals, but rather to encourage respectfully and deliberately thought-out interface design.

3.2 CRUST Considerations

We're getting closer to function internals, which will be discussed at length in Chapter 4. Before we do so, we need to address a few more concerns on the component level. This section explores how to keep components simple by following the CRUST principle outlined in Chapter 2.

3.2.1 Do Repeat Yourself, Occasionally

The DRY principle (Don't Repeat Yourself) is one of the best regarded principles in software development, and rightly so. It prompts us to write a loop when we could write a hundred print statements. It makes us create reusable functions so that we don't end up having to maintain several instances of the same piece of code. It also questions the need for slight permutations of what's virtually the same piece of code repeated over and over across our codebases.

---

1 In A/B testing, a form of user testing, a small portion of users are presented with a different experience than that used for the general user base. We then track engagement among the two groups, and if the engagement is higher for the users with the new experience, then we might go ahead and present that to our entire user base. It is an effective way of reducing risk when we want to modify our user experience, by testing our assumptions in small experiments before we introduce changes to the majority of our users.

When taken to the extreme, though, DRY is harmful and hinders development. Our mission to find the right abstractions will be cut short if we are ever vigilant in our quest to suppress any and all repetition. When it comes to finding abstractions, it's almost always best to pause and reflect on whether we ought to force DRY at this moment, or should wait a while and see whether a better pattern emerges.

Being too quick to follow DRY may result in selecting the wrong abstraction. This mistake can cost us time if we realize it early enough, and cause even more damage the longer we let an undesirable abstraction loose.

In a similar fashion, blindly following DRY for even the smallest bit of code is bound to make our code harder to follow or read. Merging two sides of a regular expression that was optimized for readability (a rare sight in the world of regular expressions) will almost certainly make it harder to read and correctly infer its purpose. Is following DRY truly worthwhile in cases like this?

The whole point of DRY is to write concise code, improving readability in turn. When the more concise piece of code results in a program that's harder to read than what we had, DRY was probably a bad idea, a solution to a problem we didn't yet have (not in this particular piece of code, not yet anyway). To stay sane, it's necessary to take software development advice with a grain of salt, as we'll discuss in Section 3.3.4, "Applying Context," on page 62.

Most often, DRY is the correct approach. But in some cases, DRY might not be appropriate, such as when it yields trivial gains at the expense of readability or when it hinders our ability to find better abstractions. We can always come back to our piece of code and sculpt pieces away, making it more DRY. This is typically easier than trying to decouple bits of code we've mistakenly made DRY, which is why sometimes it's best to wait before we commit to this principle.

3.2.2 Feature Isolation

We've discussed interface design at great length, but we haven't touched on deciding when to split a module into smaller pieces. In modern application architectures, having certain modules may be required by conventional practices. For instance, a web application made up of multiple views may require that each view is its own component. This limitation shouldn't, however, stop us from breaking the internal implementation of the view into several smaller components. These smaller components might be reused in other views or components, tested on their own, and better isolated than they might have otherwise been if they were tightly coupled to their parent view.

Even when the smaller component isn't being reused anywhere else, and perhaps not even tested on its own, moving it to a different file is still worthwhile. Why? Because we're removing the complexity that makes up the child component from its parent virtually for free. We're paying only a cheap indirect cost, as the child component is now referenced as a dependency of its parent instead of being inlined. When we split the internals of a large component into several children, we're chopping up its internal complexity and ending up with several simple components. The complexity didn't dissipate; it's subtly hidden away in the interrelationships between these child components and their parent. But that's now the biggest concern in the parent module, whereas each of the smaller modules doesn't need to know much about these relationships.

Chopping up internals doesn't work only for view components and their children. That said, view components are a great example that might help us visualize the way complexity can remain flat across a component system, regardless of how deep we go, instead of being contained in a large component with little structure and a high level of complexity or coupling. This is akin to looking at the universe on a macroscopic level and then taking a closer look, until we get to the atomic level, and then beyond. Each layer has its own complexities and intricacies waiting to be discovered, but the complexity is spread across the layers rather than clustered on any one particular layer. The spread reduces the amount of complexity we have to observe and deal with on any given layer.

Speaking of layers, it is at this stage of the design process that you might want to consider defining different layers for your application. You might be accustomed to having models, views, and controllers in MVC applications, or actions, reducers, and selectors in Redux applications. Maybe you should think of implementing a service layer where all the business logic occurs, or perhaps a persistence layer where all the caching and persistent storage takes place.

When we're not dealing with modules that we ought to shape in a certain way (like views), but modules that can be composed any which way we choose (like services), we should consider whether new features belong in an existing module or in an entirely new module. When we have a module that wraps a Markdown parsing library, adding functionality such as support for emoji expansions, and want an API that can take the resulting HTML and strip out certain tags and attributes, should we add that functionality to the Markdown module or put it in a separate module?

On the one hand, having it in the Markdown module would save us the trouble of importing both modules when we want the sanitization functionality. On the other hand, in quite a few cases we might have HTML that didn't come from Markdown parsing but that we still want to sanitize. A solution that's often effective in these cases is putting the HTML sanitization functionality into its own module, but consuming it in the Markdown module for convenience. This way, consumers of the Markdown module always get sanitized output, and those who want to sanitize a piece of HTML directly can do so as well. We could always make sanitization opt-in (or better yet, opt-out) for the Markdown module, if the feature isn't always what's needed by consumers of that interface.

It can be tempting to create a *utilities.js* module where we deposit all of our functionality that doesn't belong anywhere else. When we move onto a new project, we tend to want some of this functionality once again, so we might copy the relevant parts over to the new module. Here we'd be breaking the DRY principle, because instead of reusing the same bits of code, we're creating a new module that's a duplicate of what we had. Worse yet, over time we'll eventually modify the *utilities.js* component, and at that point the new project would not contain the same functionality anymore.

The low-hanging fruit here would be to create a *lib* directory instead of a single *utilities.js* module, and to place each independent piece of functionality into its own module. Naturally, some of these pieces of functionality will depend on other utility functions, but we'll be better off importing those bits from another module than keeping everything in the same file. Each small file clearly indicates utility as well as the other bits it relies on, and can be tested and documented individually. More importantly, when the utility grows in scope, file size, and complexity, it will remain manageable because we've isolated it early. In contrast, if we kept everything in the same file but then one of the utilities grew considerably, we'd have to pull the functionality into a different module. At that point, our code might be coupled with other utilities in subtle ways that might make the migration to a multimodule architecture a bit harder than it should be.

Were we to truly embrace a modular architecture, we might go the extra mile after promoting each utility to its own module. We could start by identifying utility modules we'd like to reuse—for example, a function used to generate slugs such as this-is-a-slug based on an arbitrary string that might have spaces, accents, punctuation, and symbols, besides alphanumeric characters. Then we could move the module to its own directory, along with documentation and tests, register any dependencies in *package.json*, and publish it to an npm registry. In doing so, we'd be honoring DRY across projects. When we update the slugging package while working on our latest project, older projects would also benefit from new functionality and bug fixes.

This approach can be taken as far as we consider necessary: as long as we'd benefit from a piece of functionality being reusable across our projects, we can make it so, adding tests and documentation along the way. Note that hypermodularity offers diminishing returns; the more we take modularity to the extreme, the more time we'll have to spend on documentation and testing. If we intend to release each line of code we develop as its own well-documented and well-tested package, we'll be spending quite some time on tasks not directly related to developing features or fixing bugs. As always, use your own judgment to decide how far to take modular structures.

When a piece of code is not complex and rather small, it's usually not worth creating a module for. That code might be better kept in a function on the module where it's consumed, or inlined every time. Such short pieces of code tend to change and branch out, often necessitating slightly different implementations in different portions of our codebase. Because the amount of code is so small, it's hardly worth our time to figure out a way to generalize the snippet of code for all or even most use cases. Chances are we'd end up with something more complex than if we just inlined the functionality to begin with.

When a piece of code is complex enough to warrant its own module, that doesn't immediately make creating a package for it worthwhile. External modules often involve a little bit more maintenance work, in exchange for being reusable across codebases and offering a cleaner interface that's properly documented. Take into consideration the amount of time you'll have to spend extricating the module and writing documentation, and whether that's worth the effort. Extricating the module will be challenging if it has dependencies on other parts of the codebase it belongs to, since those would have to be extricated as well. Writing documentation is typically not something we do for every module of a codebase. However, we have to document modules when they're their own package, since we can't expect other potential consumers to effectively decide whether they'll be using a package without having read exactly what it does or how to use it.

3.2.3 Trade-Offs When Designing Internals

When we're designing the internals of a module, keeping our priorities in order is key: the goal is to do what consumers of this module need. That goal has several aspects to it, so let's visit them in order of importance.

First off, we need to design the right interface. A complicated interface will frustrate and drive off consumers, making our module irrelevant or, at best, a pain to work with. Having an elegant or fast implementation will be of little help if our reluctant consumers have trouble leveraging the interface in front of them. A programming interface is so much more than beautiful packaging making up for a mediocre present. For consumers, the interface should be all there is. Having a simple, concise, and intuitive interface will, in turn, drive down complexity in code written by consumers. Thus, the number one step toward our goal is to find the best possible interface that caters to the needs and wants of its consumers.

Second, we need to develop something that works precisely as advertised and documented. An elegant and fast implementation that doesn't do what it's supposed to is no good to our consumers. Promising the right interface is great, but it needs to be backed up by an implementation that can deliver on the promises we make through the interface. Only then can consumers trust the code we write.

Third, the implementation should be as simple as possible. The simpler our code, the easier it will be for us to introduce changes to it without having to rewrite the existing implementation. Note that simple doesn't necessarily mean terse. For example, a simple implementation might indulge in long but descriptive variable names and a few comments explaining why code is written the way it is. Besides the ability to introduce changes, simple code is easier to follow when debugging errors, when new developers interact with the piece of software, or when the original implementors need to interact with it after a long period of time without having to worry about it. Implementation simplicity comes in third, but only after a proper interface that works as expected.

Fourth, the internals should be as performant as possible. Granted, some measure of performance is codified in producing something that works well, because something that's too slow to be considered reliable would be unacceptable to consumers. Beyond that, performance falls to the fourth place in our list of desirable traits. Performance is a feature, to be treated as such, and we should favor simplicity and readability over speed. There are some exceptions, where performance is of the utmost importance, even at the cost of producing suboptimal interfaces and code that's not all that easy to read. But in these cases, we should at least strive to heavily comment the relevant pieces of code so that it's abundantly clear why the code had to be written the way it was.

Flexibility, other than that afforded by writing simple code and providing an appropriate interface, has no place in satisfying the needs of our consumers. Trying to anticipate needs is more often than not going to result in more complexity, code, and time spent, with hardly anything to show for it in terms of improving the consumer's experience.

3.3 Pruning a Module

Much like modern web development, module design is never truly done. In this section, we'll visit a few topics that'll get you thinking about the long half-life of components, and how to design and build our components so that they don't cause us much trouble after we've finished actively developing them.

3.3.1 Error Handling, Mitigation, Detection, and Solving

While working on software development, we'll invariably need to spend time analyzing the root cause of subtle bugs that seem impossible to hunt down. Only after spending invaluable time will we figure out that the bug was caused by a small difference in program state that we had taken for granted. That small difference snowballed through our application's logic flow and into the serious issue we just had to hunt down.

We can't prevent this from happening over and over—not entirely. Unexpected bugs will always find their way to the surface. Maybe we don't control a piece of software that interacts with our own code in an unexpected way, which works well until it doesn't anymore because of a problem in the data. Maybe the problem is merely a validation function that isn't working the way it's supposed to, allowing data to flow through the system in a shape that it shouldn't; but by the time it causes an error, we'll have to spend quite some time figuring out that, indeed, the culprit is a bug in our validation function, triggered by a malformed kind of input that was undertested. Since the bug is completely unrelated to the error's stack trace information, we might spend a few hours hunting down and identifying the issue.

What we can do is mitigate the risk of bugs by writing more predictable code or improving test coverage. We can also become more proficient at debugging.

In the predictable code arena, we must be sure to handle every expected error. When it comes to error handling, we typically will bubble the error up the stack and handle it at the top, by logging it to an analytics tracker, to standard output, or to a database. When using a function call that we know might throw (for example, JSON.parse on user input) we should wrap it with try/catch and handle the error, again bubbling it up to the consumer if our inability to proceed with the function logic is final. If we're dealing with conventional callbacks that have an error argument, let's handle the error in a guard clause. Whenever we have a promise chain, make sure to add a .catch reaction to the end of the chain that handles any errors occurring in the chain. In the case of async functions, we could use try/catch or, alternatively, we can add a .catch reaction to the result of invoking the async function. While leveraging streams or other conventional event-based interfaces, make sure to bind an error event handler. Proper error handling should all but eliminate the chance of expected errors crippling our software. Simple code is predictable. Thus, following the suggestions in Chapter 4 will aid us in reducing the odds of encountering unexpected errors as well.

Test coverage can help detect unexpected errors. If we have simple and predictable code, it's harder for unexpected errors to seep through the seams. Tests can further abridge the gap by enlarging the corpus of expected errors. When we add tests, preventable errors are codified by test cases and fixtures. When tests are comprehensive enough, we might run into unexpected errors in testing and fix them. Since we've already codified those errors in a test case, they can't happen again (a test regression) without our test suite failing.

Regardless of how determined we are to develop simple, predictable, and thoroughly tested programs, we're still bound to run into bugs we hadn't expected. Tests exist mostly to prevent regressions, preventing us from running once again into bugs we've already fixed; and to prevent expected mistakes, errors we think might arise if we were to tweak our code in incorrect ways. Tests can do little to prognosticate and prevent software bugs from happening, however.

This brings us to the inevitability of debugging. Using step-through debugging, inspecting application state as we step through the code leading to a bug, is a useful tool, but it will not help us debug our code any faster than we can diagnose exactly what is going on.

To become truly effective debuggers, we must understand how the software we depend on works internally. If we don't understand the internals of something, we're effectively dealing with a black box in which anything can happen from our perspective. This adventure is left as an exercise for you, who is better equipped to determine how to obtain a higher understanding of the way your dependencies truly work. Reading the documentation might suffice, but this is rarely the case. Perhaps you should opt to download the source code from GitHub and give it a read. Maybe you're more of a hands-on kind of person and prefer to try your hand at making your own knock-off of a library you depend on, in order to understand how it works. Regardless of the path you take, the next time you run into an unexpected error related to a dependency that you're more intimately familiar with, you'll have an easier time identifying the root cause, since you'll be aware of the limitations and common pitfalls of what was previously mostly a black box to you. Documentation can take us only so far in understanding how something works under the hood, which is what's required when tracking down unexpected errors.

3.3.2 Documentation as an Art

It is true: in the hard times of tracking down and fixing an unexpected error, documentation often plays a diminished role. Documentation is, however, often fundamental when trying to understand how a piece of code works, and this can't be underestimated. Public interface documentation underscores readable code, and is useful not only as a guide for consumers to draw from for usage examples and advanced configuration options that may aid them when coming up with their own designs, but also for implementors as a reference of exactly what consumers are promised and, hence, ultimately expect.

In this section, we're talking about documentation in its broadest possible sense. We've discussed public interface documentation, but tests and code comments are also documentation in their own way. Even variable or function names should be considered a kind of documentation. Tests act as programmatic documentation for the kinds of inputs and outputs we expect from our public interfaces. In the case of integration tests, they describe the minimum acceptable behavior of our application, such as allowing users to log in providing an email and a password. Code comments serve as documentation for implementors to understand why code looks the way it does, indicate areas of improvement, and often refer the reader to links offering further details on a bug fix that might not look all that elegant at first sight. Descriptive variable names can, cumulatively, save the reader considerable time when explicit names like `products` are preferred over vague and ambiguous names like `data`. The same applies to function names: we should prefer names like `aggregate SessionsPerDay` over something shorter but unclear such as `get Stats`.

Getting into the habit of treating every bit of code and the structure around it (formal documentation, tests, comments) as documentation itself is only logical. Those who will be reading our code in the future—developers looking to further their understanding of how the code works, and implementors doing the same in order to extend or repair a portion of functionality—rely on our ability to convey a concise message about the way the interface and its internals work.

Why would we not, then, strive to take advantage of every variable, property, and function name; every component name; every test case; and every bit of formal documentation to explain precisely what our programs do, how they do it, and why we opted for certain trade-offs?

In this sense, we should consider documentation to be the art of taking every possible opportunity to clearly and deliberately express the intent and reasoning of all the aspects of our modules.

I don't mean to say we should flood consumers and implementors alike until they drown in a tumultuous stream of never-ending documentation. On the contrary, only by being deliberate in our messaging can we strike the right balance and describe the public interface in formal documentation, describe notable usage examples in our test cases, and explain abnormalities in comments.

Following a holistic approach to documentation, through which we're aware of who might be reading what, and what should be directed to whom, should result in easy-to-follow prose that's not ambiguous as to usage or best practices, nor fragmented, nor repetitive. Interface documentation should be limited to how the interface works and is rarely the place to discuss design choices, which can be relayed to architecture or design documentation, and later linked in relevant places. Code comments are great for explaining why, or linking to a bug fixed in their vicinity, but they aren't usually the best place to discuss why an interface looks the way it does. This is better left to architecture documentation or our issue tracker of choice. Dead code should definitely not be kept around in comment blocks, as it does nothing but confuse the reader, and is better kept in feature branches or Git stashes, but off the trunk of source control.

Tom Preston-Werner wrote about the notion of README-driven development as a way of designing an interface by first describing it in terms of how it would be used. This is generally more effective than test-driven design (TDD), where we'll often find ourselves rewriting the same bits of code over and over before we realize we wanted to produce a different API to begin with. The way README-driven design is supposed to work is self-descriptive; we begin by creating a README file and writing our interface's documentation. We can start with the most common use cases, inputs, and desired outputs, as described in Section 2.1.2, "API First," on page 23, and grow our interface from there. Doing this in a README file instead of a module leaves us an itsy bit more detached from an eventual implementation, but the essence is the same. The largest difference is that, much like TDD, we'd be committing to writing a README file over and over before we settle for a desirable API. Regardless, both API-first and README-driven design offer significant advantages over diving straight into an implementation.

3.3.3 Removing Code

A popular description of CSS as an "append-only language" implies that after a piece of CSS code has been added, it can't be removed; doing so could inadvertently break our designs because of the way the cascade works. JavaScript doesn't make it quite that hard to remove code, but it's indeed a highly dynamic language, and removing code with the certainty that nothing will break remains a bit of a challenge as well.

Naturally, modifying a module's internal implementation is easier than changing its public API, as the effects of doing so would be limited to the module's internals. Internal changes that don't affect the API are typically not observable from the outside. The exception to that rule occurs when consumers monkey-patch our interface, sometimes becoming able to observe some of our internals.[2] In this case, however, the consumer should be aware of the brittleness of monkey-patching a module they do not control, and that they do so assuming the risk of breakage.

In Section 3.1.2, "Design for Today," on page 45 we observed that the best code is no code at all, and this has implications when it comes to removing code as well. Code we never write is code we don't need to worry about deleting. The less code there is, the less code we need to maintain, the less potential bugs we have yet to uncover, and the less code we need to read, test, and deliver over mobile networks to speed-hungry humans.

As portions of our programs become stale and unused, it is best to remove them entirely instead of postponing their inevitable fate.

---

2 Monkey-patching is the intentional modification of the public interface of a component from the outside in order to add, remove, or change its functionality. Monkey-patching can be helpful when we want to change the behavior of a component that we don't control, such as a library or dependency. Patching is error-prone because we might be affecting other consumers of this API who are unaware of our patches. The API itself or its internals may also change, breaking the assumptions made about them in our patch. Although it's generally best avoided, sometimes it's the only choice at hand.

Any code we desire to keep around for reference or the possibility of reinstating it in the future can be safely preserved by source control software without the necessity of keeping it around in our codebase. Avoiding commented-out code and removing unused code as soon as possible will keep our codebase cleaner and easy to follow. When there's dead code, a developer might be uncertain as to whether this is actually in use somewhere else, and reluctant to remove it. As time passes, the theory of broken windows comes into full effect, and we'll soon have a codebase that's riddled with unused code nobody knows the purpose of or how the codebase has become so unmanageable.

Reusability plays a role in code removal. As more components depend on a module, it becomes more unlikely we'll be able to trivially remove the heavily depended-on piece of code. When a module has no connections to other modules, it can be removed from the codebase, but might still serve a purpose as its own standalone package.

3.3.4 Applying Context

Software development advice is often written in absolute terms, rarely considering context. When you bend a rule to fit your situation, you're not necessarily disagreeing with the advice; you might just have applied a different context to the same problem. The advisor may have missed that context or might have avoided it because it was inconvenient.

However convincing an eloquent piece of advice or tool might seem, always apply your own critical thinking and context first. What might work for large companies at an incredible scale, under a great load, and with their own unique set of problems, might not be suitable for your personal blogging project. What might seem like a sensible idea for a weekend hack might not be the best use of a mid-size startup's time.

Whenever you're analyzing whether a dependency, tool, or piece of advice fits your needs, always start by reading available resources and consider whether the problem being solved is one you indeed need to solve. Avoid falling into the trap of leveraging advice or tools merely because it became popular or is being hailed by a large actor.

Never overcommit to that which you're not certain fits your needs, but always experiment. It is by keeping an open mind that we can capture new knowledge, improve our understanding of the world, and innovate. This is aided by critical thinking and hindered by rushing to the newest technology without firsthand experimentation. In any case, rules are meant to be bent and broken.

Let's move to the next chapter, where we'll decipher the art of writing less-complex functions.

CHAPTER 4

Shaping Internals

Thus far we've addressed modular design and API design concerns from a high-level perspective, but avoided plunging into the deep end of implementation details. In contrast, this chapter is devoted to advice and concrete actions we can take to improve the quality of our component implementations. We'll discuss complexity, ways to remediate it, the perils of state, and how to better leverage data structures.

4.1 Internal Complexity

Every piece of code we write is a source of internal complexity, with the potential to become a large pain point for our codebase as a whole. That said, most bits of code are relatively harmless when compared to the entire corpus of our codebase, and trying to proof our code against complexity is a sure way of increasing complexity for no observable benefit. The question is, then, how do we identify the small problems before they grow into a serious threat to the maintainability of our project?

Making a conscious effort to track pieces of code that we haven't changed or interacted with in a while, and identifying whether they're simple enough to understand can help us determine whether refactoring may be in order. We could, perhaps, set a rule whereby team members should watch out for garden paths in the codebase and fix them as they are making changes in the same functional area as the affected code. When we track complexity methodically, often, and across the entire team that's responsible for a codebase, we can expect to see many small but cumulative gains in our battle against complexity.

4.1.1 Containing Nested Complexity

In JavaScript, deep nesting is one of the clearest signs of complexity. Understanding the code at any given nesting level involves understanding how the flow arrives there, the state at every level in scope, how the flow might break out of the level, and which other flows might lead to the same level. Granted, we don't always need to keep all this derived information in our memory. The problem is that, when we do, we might have to spend quite a few minutes reading and understanding the code, deriving such information, and otherwise not fixing the bug or implementing the feature that we had set out to resolve in the first place.

Nesting is the underlying source of complexity in patterns such as "callback hell," or "promise hell," in which callbacks are nested on top of one another. The complexity has little to do with spacing, although when taken to the extreme, that does make code harder to read. Instead, the complexity exists at the seams, where we need to fully understand the context in order to go deep into the callback chain and make fixes or improvements. An insidious variant of callback hell is the one where we have logic in every nesting level. This variant is coincidentally the one we can observe most often in real applications: we rarely have callbacks as depicted in the following bit of code, partly because it's immediately obvious that something is wrong. We should probably either change the API so that we get everything we need at once, or we could leverage a small library that takes care of the flow while eliminating the deep nesting we'd otherwise have in our own code:

```
getProducts(products => {
  getProductPrices(products, prices => {
    getProductDetails({ products, prices }, details => {
      // ...
    })
  })
})
```

When we have synchronous logic intermixed with asynchronous callbacks, things get more challenging. The problem here is, almost always, a coupling of concerns. When a program has a series of nested callbacks that also include logic in between, it can be a sign that we're mixing flow-control concerns with business concerns. In other words, our program would be in a better place if we kept the flow separate from the business logic. By splitting the code that purely determines the flow from the rest, we can better isolate our logic into its individual components. The flow, in turn, also becomes clearer because it's now spelled out in plain sight instead of interleaved with business concerns.

Suppose that each nesting level in a series of callbacks contains about 50 lines of code. Each function in the series needs to reference zero, one, or more variables in its parent scope. If it needs zero references to its immediate parent scope, we can safely move it up to the same scope as its parent. We can repeat this process until the function is at the highest possible level, given the variables it has to reference. When functions reference at least one variable from the parent scope, we could opt to leave them unchanged or to pass those references as parameters so that we can keep on decoupling the functions.

As we move logic into its own functions and flatten the callback chain, we'll be left with the bare flow of operations being separate from the operations themselves. Libraries like contra can help manage the flow itself, while user code worries about business logic.

4.1.2 Feature Entanglement and Tight Coupling

As a module becomes larger, it also gets easier to mistakenly collapse distinct features together by interleaving their code in such a way that it is hard to reuse each feature independently, debug and maintain them, or otherwise extricate the features from one another.

For example, if we have a feature for notifying subscribers and a feature to send notifications, we could strive to keep the features apart by clearly defining how notifications can be constructed and handed off to a different service that then sends those notifications. That way, subscriber notifications can be sent through the notification service, but given the clear separation, we won't be letting subscriber-specific notions get in the way of sending other kinds of notifications to our customers.

One way of reducing the risk of entanglement is to design features up front, being particularly on the lookout for concerns that could be componentized or otherwise clearly delineated. By doing a little work before sitting down to write code, we might avert the risks of tight coupling.

Being alert when reading old code can also be key in identifying what was previously a well-contained module that evolved to cover a broad range of concerns. We can then, over time, break these concerns into individual modules or better-isolated functions so that each concern is easier to maintain and understand separately.

Instead of trying to build a large feature all at once, we could build it from the inside out, keeping each stage of the process in functions that live at the same level instead of being deeply nested. Doing this methodically will lead to better decoupling, as we'll move away from monolithic structures and toward a more modular approach, where functions have smaller scopes and take what they need in the form of parameters.

When we'd have to repeat ourselves by passing a lot of scope variables as function parameters just to avoid nested functions, a light degree of nesting is desirable to avoid this repetition. In key functional boundaries, where our concerns go from "gather model details" to "render HTML page" to "print HTML page to PDF," nesting will invariably lead to coupling and less reusability, which is why repeating ourselves a little bit may be warranted in these cases.

4.1.3 Frameworks: The Good, the Bad, and the Ugly

Conventions are useful because they allow for better self-direction among developers, without causing lagoons of inconsistency to spread across our codebase. Chaos would ensue should we allow a team of developers too much freedom without sound design direction and conventions that dictate how different portions of an application should be shaped. A large number of conventions might hinder productivity, especially if some of our conventions appeared to work as if by magic.

When it comes to conventions, frameworks are a special case. Frameworks are packed to the brim with conventions and best practices. Some of them live in the library and tooling ecosystem around the framework, while many live in the shape our code takes when we rely on that framework. Upon adopting a framework, we're buying into its conventions and practices. Most modern JavaScript frameworks offer ways of breaking our application into small chunks, regardless of whether the framework is for the client or server.

Express has middleware and routes; AngularJS has directives, services, and controllers; React has components; and so on and so forth. These conventions and abstractions are tremendously helpful to keep complexity in check while building an application. As our components grow larger, regardless of the abstraction or framework of choice, things will get more complicated. At this moment, we usually can refactor our code into smaller components that are then wrapped with larger ones, preserving separation of concerns, and keeping complexity on a short leash.

Eventually, we'll come across requirements that don't exactly fit the mold proposed by our framework of choice. Generally, this means that the required functionality belongs on a separate layer. For example, Express in Node.js is a framework concerned with handling HTTP requests and serving responses. If one of our API endpoints needs to result in an email being sent, we could embed email-sending logic in the controller for that API endpoint. However, if an API endpoint controller is already concerned with, say, publishing blog posts, then it would be hardly right to embed email-sending logic on that same controller since it's a different concern entirely. Instead, what we could do is create a `subscribers` service component, with functionality such as `subscribe`, which adds a subscriber after verifying their email, and `notify`, which takes care of sending the emails. Taking this idea further still, perhaps most of the work in `subscribers.notify` should occur via yet another service component called `emails`, which takes care of properly configuring our email-sending capability, and also has functionality to turn would-be emails into plain `console.log` statements for quick access to the contents of the emails during debug sessions.

Having clearly defined layers is paramount to the design of effective and maintainable applications once we're past the prototyping stages. Layers can be made up of components that follow the conventions proposed by the frameworks we use, or they can be self-imposed, like the service layer discussed in the previous paragraph. Using layers, and as long as we favor function parameters over scope for context passing, we can introduce horizontal scaling by placing several orthogonal components alongside each other, without letting them run into each other's concerns.

4.2 Refactoring Complex Code

Code is ever-evolving, and we'll almost invariably end up with large projects that are not always the easiest to maintain. While we'll reserve the following couple of sections for practical recommendations to reduce complexity at an architectural level, this section focuses on reducing complexity in portions of an application that are already complex.

4.2.1 Embracing Variables over Clever Code

Complex code is predominantly shorter than it should be, and often deceitfully so. An expression that might have involved 5 to 10 short lines of code usually ends up being represented in 1 or 2 clever lines of code. The problem with clever code is that we need to expend time and energy to read it whenever its intent is not clear in our mind, which is only the case when we first write the code or right after spending considerable time analyzing it.

One of the underlying issues that can be identified when reading complex code is that it uses few variables. In the dawn of programming, memory resources were scarce, so programmers had to optimize allocation, and this often meant reusing variables and using fewer of them. In modern systems, we don't need to treat memory as a sacred, precious, and limited resource. Instead, we can focus on making programs readable to both our future selves and fellow developers.

Readability is better served by an abundance of properly named variables or functions than by sparsity. Consider the following example, part of a larger routine; a program ensures that the user is currently logged in with a valid session, and otherwise redirects the user to a login page:

```
if (
  auth !== undefined &&
  auth.token !== undefined &&
  auth.expires > Date.now()
) {
  // we have a valid token that hasn't expired yet
  return
}
```

As the routine becomes larger, we collect if statements with nonobvious or complicated clauses, such as the reason we're checking that auth has a `token` value if we're not doing anything with it here. The solution is usually to add a comment explaining the reason this check exists. In this case, the comment tells us this is a valid token that hasn't expired. We could turn that comment into code, and simplify the `if` statement in the process, by creating a small function that breaks down the conditional, as shown next:

```
function hasValidToken(auth) {
  if (auth === undefined || auth.token === undefined) {
    return false
  }
  const hasNotExpiredYet = auth.expires > Date.now()
  return hasNotExpiredYet
}
```

We can now turn our `if` statement plus comment into a function call, as shown in the following bit of code. Certainly, the totality of our refactored code is a bit longer, but now it's self-descriptive. Code that describes what it does in the process of doing it doesn't require as many comments, and that's important because comments can become easily outdated. Moreover, we've extracted the long conditional in the `if` statement to a function, which keeps us more focused while parsing the codebase. If every condition or task was inline, we'd have to understand everything in order to understand how a program works. When we offload tasks and conditions to other functions, we're letting readers know they can have faith that `hasValidToken` will check for validity of the `auth` object, and the conditional becomes a lot easier to digest:

```
if (hasValidToken(auth)) {
  return
}
```

We could've used more variables without creating a function, inlining the computation of `hasValidToken` right before the `if` check. A crucial difference between the function-based refactor and the inlining solution is that we used a short-circuiting `return` statement to preemptively bail when we already knew the token was invalid.[1] However, we can't use `return` statements to bail from the snippet that computes `hasValidToken` in the following piece of code without coupling its computation to knowledge about what the routine should return for failure cases. As a result, our only options are

---

1 In the example, we immediately return `false` when the token isn't present.

tightly coupling the inline subroutine to its containing function, or using a logical or ternary operator in the intermediate steps of the inlined computation:

```
const hasToken = auth === undefined || auth.token === undefined
const hasValidToken = hasToken && auth.expires > Date.now()
if (hasValidToken) {
  return
}
```

Both of these options have their downsides. If we couple the `return` statements with the parent function, we'll need to be careful if we want to replicate the logic elsewhere, as the `return` statements and possibly their logic will have to adapt as well. If we decide to use ternary operators as a way of short-circuiting, we'll end up with logic that might be as complex as the code we originally had in the `if` statement.

Using a function not only avoids these two problems, thanks to the ability to `return` intermediate results, but also defers reasoning about its contents until we actually need to understand how tokens are checked for validity.

Although moving conditionals to a `function` might sound like a trivial task, this approach is at the heart of modular design. It is by composing small bits of complexity using several additive functions that we can build large applications that are less straining to read. A large pool of mostly trivial functions can add up to a veritable codebase in which each bit of code is relatively isolated and easy to understand, provided we trust that functions do what their names say they do. In this vein, it is of utmost importance to think long and deep about the name of every function, every variable, and every package, directory, or data structure we conceive.

When used deliberately and extensively, early returns—sometimes referred to as *guard clauses* or *short-circuits*—can be unparalleled when it comes to making an application as readable as possible. Let's explore this concept in further detail.

4.2.2 Guard Clauses and Branch Flipping

When we have a long branch inside a conditional statement, chances are we're doing something wrong. Pieces of code like the following are commonplace in real-world applications, with a long success case branch taking up significant amounts of code while having several else branches sprinkled near the end that would log an error, throw, return, or otherwise perform a failure-handling action:

```
if (response) {
  if (!response.errors) {
    // ... use `response`
  } else {
    return false
  }
} else {
  return false
}
```

In the example, we're optimizing readability for the success case, while the failure handling is relegated to the very end of our piece of code. There are several problems with this approach. For one, we have to indulge in unnecessary nesting of every success condition, or otherwise put them all in a huge conditional statement. Although it's rather easy to understand the success case, things can get tricky when we're trying to debug programs like this, because we need to keep the conditionals in our head the whole time we're reading the program.

A better alternative is to flip the conditionals, placing all failure-handling statements near the top. Though counterintuitive at first, this approach has several benefits. It reduces nesting and eliminates else branches, while promoting failure handling to the top of our code. This has the added benefit that we'll become more aware of error handling and naturally gravitate toward thinking about the failure cases first. This is a great trait to have when doing application development, where forgetting to handle a failure case might result in an inconsistent experience for end users with a hard-to-trace error on top. The following example illustrates the early exit approach:

```
if (!response) {
  return false
}
if (response.errors) {
  return false
}
// ... use `response`
```

As stated previously, this early-exit approach is often referred to as *guard clauses*. One of their biggest benefits is that we can learn all the failure cases upon reading the first few lines of a function or piece of code. We're not limited to `return` statements; we could `throw` errors in a promise-based context or in an async function, and in callback chaining contexts we might opt for a `done(error)` callback followed by a `return` statement.

Another benefit of guard clauses is almost implicit: given that they're placed near the top of a function, we have quick access to its parameters, we can better understand how the function validates its inputs, and we can more effectively decide whether we need to add new guard clauses to improve validation rules.

Guard clauses don't tell the reader everything they need to know that might go wrong when calling a function, but they provide a peek into expected immediate failure cases. Other things that might go wrong lie in the implementation details of the function. Perhaps we use a different service or library to fulfill the bulk of our function's task, and that service or library comes with its own set of nested guard clauses and potential failure cases that will bubble up all the way to our own function's outcome.

4.2.3 An Interdependency Pyramid

Writing straightforward code is not all that different from writing other straightforward text. Text is often arranged in paragraphs, which are somewhat comparable with functions; we can consider their input to be the reader's knowledge and everything else they've read so far in the text, and the output to be what the reader gets out of the paragraph.

Within a book chapter or any other piece of long-form text, paragraphs are organized in a sequential manner, allowing the reader time to digest each paragraph before jumping onto the next. The logical sequence is very much intentional: without a coherent sequencing, it would be nearly impossible to make sense of a text. Thus, writers optimize for making sure concepts are introduced before they're discussed, providing context to the reader.

Function expressions such as the one in the next snippet won't be assigned to the variable binding until the line containing the assignment is evaluated. Until then, the variable binding exists in the scope, thanks to hoisting, but it is `undefined` until the assignment statement is evaluated:

```
double(6) // TypeError: double is not a function
var double = function(x) {
  return x * 2
}
```

Furthermore, if we're dealing with a let or const binding, then TDZ semantics produce an error if we reference the binding at all before the variable declaration statement is reached:

```
double(6) // TypeError: double is not defined
const double = function(x) {
  return x * 2
}
```

Function declarations like the one in the following snippet, in contrast, are hoisted to the top of the scope. This means we can reference them anywhere in our code:

```
double(6) // 12
function double(x) {
  return x * 2
}
```

Now, I mentioned that text is written sequentially, and that writers avoid surprises by presenting concepts before discussing them. Establishing a context in a program is a different endeavor, however. If we have a module that has the goal of rendering a chart with user engagement statistics, the top of the function should address things the reader already knows—namely, the high-level flow for what the rendering function is meant to do: analyze the data, construct some data views, and model that data into something we can feed into a visualization library that then renders the desired chart.

What we have to avoid is jumping directly into unimportant functions such as a data-point label formatter, or the specifics of the data modeling. By keeping only the high-level flow near the top, and the specifics toward the end, complex functionality can be designed in such a way that readers experience a zoomed-out overview of the functionality at first, and as they read the code, they uncover the details of the way this chart was implemented.

In a concrete sense, this means we should present functions in a codebase in the order that they'll be read by the consumer (a first-in, first-out queue), and not in the execution order (a last-in, first-out stack). Computers do as they're told and dig ever deeper into the flow, executing the most deeply nested routines before jumping out of a series of subroutines and executing the next line. But this is an unfruitful way for humans to read a codebase, given we're ill-suited to keeping all that state in our heads.

Perhaps a more specific analogy for this kind of spiraling approach can be found in newspaper articles; the author typically offers a title that describes an event at the highest possible level, and then follows up with a lead paragraph that summarizes what happened, again at a high level. The body of the article starts also at a high level, carefully avoiding to spook the reader with too many details. It is only midway through the article that we'll start finding details about the event that, aided by the context set forth at the beginning of the article, can give us a complete picture of what transpired.

Given the stack-based nature of programming, it's not that easy to naturally approach programs as if they were newspaper articles. We can, however, defer execution of implementation details to other functions or subroutines, and thanks to hoisting, we can place those subroutines after their higher-level counterparts. In doing so, we're organizing our programs in a way that invites readers in, shows them a few high-level hints, and then gradually unveils the spooky details of the way a feature is implemented.

4.2.4 Extracting Functions

Deliberate, pyramidal structures that deal with higher-level concerns near the top and switch to more-specific problems as we go deeper into the inner workings of a system work wonders in keeping complexity on a tight leash. Such structures are particularly powerful because they break complex items into their own individual units near the flat bottom of the system, avoiding a complicated interweaving of concerns that are fuzzied together, becoming indistinguishable from one another over time.

Pushing anything that gets in the way of the current flow to the bottom of a function is an effective way of streamlining readability. As an example, imagine that we have a nontrivial mapper inline, in the heart of a function. In the following code snippet, we're mapping the users into user models, as we often need to do when preparing JSON responses for API calls:

```
function getUserModels(done) {
  findUsers((err, users) => {
    if (err) {
      done(err)
      return
```

```
    }

    const models = users.map(user => {
      const { name, email } = user
      const model = { name, email }
      if (user.type.includes('admin')) {
        model.admin = true
      }
      return model
    })

    done(null, models)
  })
}
```

Now compare that to the following bit of code, where we extract the mapping function and shove it out of the way. Given that the mapping function doesn't need any of the scope from getUserModels, we can pull it out of that scope entirely, without needing to place toUserModel at the bottom of the getUserModels function. This means we can now also reuse toUserModel in other routines. We don't have to wonder whether the function actually depends on any of the containing scope's context anymore, and getUserModels is now focused on the higher-level flow where we find users, map them to their models, and return them:

```
function getUserModels(done) {
  findUsers((err, users) => {
    if (err) {
      done(err)
      return
    }

    const models = users.map(toUserModel)

    done(null, models)
  })
}

function toUserModel(user) {
  const { name, email } = user
  const model = { name, email }
  if (user.type.includes('admin')) {
    model.admin = true
  }
  return model
}
```

Furthermore, if additional work needed to be done between the mapping and the callback, that work could also be moved into another small function that wouldn't get in the way of our higher-level getUserModels function.

A similar case occurs when we have a variable that's defined based on a condition, as shown in the next snippet. Bits of code like this can distract the reader away from the core purpose of a function, to the point where it's often ignored or glossed over:

```
// ...
let website = null
if (user.details) {
  website = user.details.website
} else if (user.website) {
  website = user.website
}
// ...
```

It's best to refactor this kind of assignment into a function, like the one shown next. Note that we include a user parameter so that we can push the function out of the scope chain where we've originally defined the user object, and at the same time go from a let binding to a const binding. When reading this piece of code later down the line, the benefit of const is that we'll know the binding won't change. With let, we can't be certain that bindings won't change over time, adding to the pile of things the reader should be watching out for when trying to understand the algorithm:

```
// ...
const website = getUserWebsite(user)
// ...

function getUserWebsite(user) {
  if (user.details) {
    return user.details.website
  }
  if (user.website) {
    return user.website
  }
  return null
}
```

Regardless of your flavor of choice when it comes to variable binding, bits of code that select a slice of application state are best shoved away from the relevant logic that will use this selected state to perform an action. This way, we're not distracted by concerns about how state is selected, instead of focusing on the action that our application logic is trying to carry out.

When we want to name an aspect of a routine without adding a comment, we could create a function to host that functionality. Doing so not only gives a name to what the algorithm is doing, but also allows us to push that code out of the way, leaving behind only the high-level description of what's going to happen.

4.2.5 Flattening Nested Callbacks

Codebases with asynchronous code flows often fall into callback hell; each callback creates a new level of indentation, making code harder and harder to read as we approach the deep end of the asynchronous flow chain:

```
a(function () {
  b(function () {
    c(function () {
      d(function () {
        console.log('hi!')
      })
    })
  })
})
```

The foremost problem with this kind of structure is scope inheritance. In the deepest callback, passed to the g function, we've inherited the combined scopes of all the parent callbacks. As functions become larger, and more variables are bound into each of these scopes, it becomes ever more challenging to understand one of the callbacks in isolation from its parents.

This kind of coupling can be reverted by naming the callbacks and placing them all in the same nesting level. Named functions may be reused in other parts of our component, or exported to be used elsewhere. In the following example, we've eliminated up to three levels of unnecessary nesting, and by eliminating nesting, we've made the scope for each function more explicit:

```
a(a1)
function a1() {
  b(b1)
}
function b1() {
  c(c1)
}
```

```
function c1() {
  d(d1)
}
function d1() {
  console.log('hi!')
}
```

When we do need some of the variables that existed in the parent scope, we can explicitly pass them on to the next callback in the chain. The following example passes an arrow function to d, as opposed to passing the d1 callback directly. When executed, the arrow function ends up calling d1 anyway, but now it has the additional parameters we needed. These parameters can come from anywhere, and we can do this throughout the chain, while keeping it all in the same indentation level:

```
a(a1)
function a1() {
  b(b1)
}
function b1() {
  c(c1)
}
function c1() {
  d(() => d1('hi!'))
}
function d1(salute) {
  console.log(salute) // <- 'hi!'
}
```

Now, this could also be resolved using a library such as async, which simplifies the flattened chaining process by establishing patterns. The async.series method accepts an array of task functions. When called, the first task is executed, and async waits until the next callback is invoked before jumping onto the next task. When all tasks have been executed, or an error arises in one of the tasks, the completion callback in the second argument passed to async.series is executed. In the following illustrative example, each of the three tasks is executed in series, one at a time, waiting a second before each task signals its own completion. Lastly, the 'done!' message is printed to the console:

```
async.series([
  next => setTimeout(() => next(), 1000),
  next => setTimeout(() => next(), 1000),
  next => setTimeout(() => next(), 1000)
], err => console.log(err ? 'failed!' : 'done!'))
```

Libraries like `async` come with several ways of mixing and matching asynchronous code flows, in series or concurrent, allowing us to pass variables between callbacks without having to nest together entire asynchronous flows.

Naturally, callbacks aren't the only asynchronous flow pattern that might end up in hell. Promises can end up in this state just as easily, as shown in this contrived snippet:

```
Promise.resolve(1).then(() =>
  Promise.resolve(2).then(() =>
    Promise.resolve(3).then(() =>
      Promise.resolve(4).then(value => {
        console.log(value) // <- 4
      })
    )
  )
)
```

A similar piece of code that wouldn't be affected by the nesting problem is shown next. Here, we're taking advantage of promises behaving in a tree-like manner. We don't necessarily need to attach reactions onto the last promise, and instead, we can return those promises so that the chaining can always occur at the top level, allowing us to avoid any and all scope inheritance:

```
Promise.resolve(1)
  .then(() => Promise.resolve(2))
  .then(() => Promise.resolve(3))
  .then(() => Promise.resolve(4))
  .then(value => {
    console.log(value) // <- 4
  })
```

Similarly, using `async` functions can turn what was previously a promise-based flow and turn it into something that can be mapped to our own mental model of the program's execution flow. The following bit of code is similar to the preceding snippet, but uses `async/await` instead:

```
async function main() {
  await Promise.resolve(1)
  await Promise.resolve(2)
  await Promise.resolve(3)
  const value = await Promise.resolve(4)
  console.log(value) // <- 4
}
```

4.2.6 Factoring Similar Tasks

We've already discussed at length why creating abstractions isn't always the best way of reducing complexity in an application. Abstractions can be particularly damaging when created too early: at the time, we might not have enough information about the shape and requirements for other components that we might want to hide behind the abstraction layer. Over time, we might end up aggressively shaping components only so that they fit the abstraction, which could have been avoided by not settling for an abstraction too early.

When we do avoid creating abstractions prematurely, we'll start noticing functions that have an uncanny resemblance to the shape of similar functions. Maybe the flow is identical, maybe the output is similar, or maybe all that really changes is we're accessing an attribute named `href` in one case and an attribute named `src` in another case.

Consider the case of an HTML crawler that needs to pull out snippets of an HTML page and reuse them later in a different context. Among other things, this crawler needs to take relative resource locators like `/weekly` and resolve them to absolute endpoints like `https://ponyfoo.com/weekly`, depending on the origin of the resource. This way, the HTML snippets can then be repurposed on other mediums, such as on a different origin or a PDF file, without breaking the end-user experience.

The following code takes a piece of HTML and transforms `a[href]` and `img[src]` into absolute endpoints by using the `$` jQuery-like DOM utility library:

```
function absolutizeHtml(html, origin) {
  const $dom = $(html)
  $dom.find('a[href]').each(function () {
    const $element = $(this)
    const href = $element.attr('href')
    const absolute = absolutize(href, origin)
    $element.attr('href', absolute)
  })
  $dom.find('img[src]').each(function () {
    const $element = $(this)
    const src = $element.attr('src')
    const absolute = absolutize(src, origin)
    $element.attr('src', absolute)
  })
```

```
    return $dom.html()
  }
```

Because the function is small, it'd be perfectly acceptable to keep absolutizeHtml as is. However, if we later decide to add iframe[src], script[src], and link[href] to the list of attributes that might contain endpoints we want to transform, we'll probably want to avoid having five copies of the same routine. That's more likely to be confusing and result in changes being made to one of them without being mirrored in the other cases, increasing complexity.

The following bit of code keeps all attributes we want to transform in an array, and abstracts the repeated bit of code so that it's reused for every tag and attribute:

```
const attributes = [
  ['a', 'href'],
  ['img', 'src'],
  ['iframe', 'src'],
  ['script', 'src'],
  ['link', 'href']
]

function absolutizeHtml(html, origin) {
  const $dom = $(html)
  attributes.forEach(absolutizeAttribute)
  return $dom.html()

  function absolutizeAttribute([ tag, property ]) {
    $dom.find(`${ tag }[${ property }]`).each(function () {
      const $element = $(this)
      const value = $element.attr(property)
      const absolute = absolutize(value, origin)
      $element.attr(property, absolute)
    })
  }
}
```

A similar situation occurs when we have a concurrent flow that remains more or less constant across multiple functions. In this case, we might want to consider keeping the flow in its own function, and passing a callback for the actual processing logic that is different in each case.

In other cases, we might notice that a few different components all need the same piece of functionality. Commenting features often fall into this case, where different components such as user profiles, projects, or artifacts might need the ability to receive, show, edit, and delete comments. This case can be interesting because the business requirement is not always identified up front, and we might embed the child feature into the parent component before realizing it'd be useful to extract the feature so that it can be reused in other parent components. While this sounds obvious in hindsight, it's not always clear when we'll need to reuse functionality somewhere else. Keeping every aspect of functionality isolated just in case we need to reuse any can be costly in terms of time and development effort.

More often than not, however, abstractions can end up complicating matters. The trade-off might not be worth it because the code becomes much harder to read, or the underlying code might not be mature enough yet. Maybe we don't know what special requirements we may end up with for other objects adopting similar functionality, meaning we're not comfortable creating an abstraction that could lead to unforeseen problems in the future.

Whenever we are uncertain about whether an abstraction is up to muster, it pays to go back to the original piece of code we had before introducing the abstraction, and comparing the two pieces. Is the new piece easier to understand, modify, and consume? Would that still be the case as a newcomer? Try to consider how the outcome of those questions would change if you hadn't looked at this code in a while. Ask your coworkers for their opinion, too; because they haven't seen that code yet and may end up having to consume it, they're great candidates to help decide which approach is better.

4.2.7 Slicing Large Functions

Consider breaking what would otherwise inevitably be a single large function into smaller functions. These may be organized by splitting functionality by steps or by each aspect of the same task. All of these functions should still always rely on guard clauses to do all of our error checking up front, ensuring that state is constrained by what we allow it to be at each point in time.

The overall structure of your typical function should begin with guard clauses, making sure the input we receive is what we expect: enforcing required parameters, their correct data types, correct data ranges, and so on. If these inputs are malformed, we should bail immediately. This ensures that we don't work with inputs we're unprepared to deal with, and ensures that the consumers get an error message explaining the root reason for not getting the results they expect (as opposed to a message that might involve debugging work), such as `undefined is not a function` caused by trying to call an input that was supposed to be a function but wasn't, or was supposed to result in our routine finding a function, but didn't.

Once we know the inputs are well formed, data processing can begin. We'll transform the inputs, map them to the output we want to produce, and return that output. Here we have the opportunity to break the function into several pieces. Each aspect of the transformation of inputs into output is potentially its own function. The way of reducing complexity in a function is not by collapsing hundreds of lines of code into tens of complicated lines of code. Instead, we can move each of these long pieces of code into individual functions that deal with only one aspect of the data. Those functions can then also be hoisted out of our function and onto its parent scope, showing that there wasn't a reason that a particular aspect of transforming the inputs had to be coupled to the entire function doing the transformation.

Each aspect of a transformation operation can be analyzed and moved into its own function. The smaller function may take a few of the inputs in the larger function, or perhaps some of the intermediate values that were produced in the larger function. It can then conduct its own input sanitization, and be broken apart even further. The process of identifying aspects of an operation that can be recursively compartmentalized and moved into their own functions is highly effective because it allows for dauntingly large functions to be broken into simpler pieces that aren't as daunting to refactor.

At first, we can identify the three or four largest aspects of a function, and break those apart. The first part might involve filtering out the parts of the input we're not interested in, the second might involve mapping that into something else, and the third part might involve merging all of the data together. Once we've identified each aspect of the function, we might break those into their own functions, with their own inputs and output. Subsequently, we can do this for each of those smaller functions.

We can keep doing this for as long as there's the opportunity for the functions to be simplified. As discussed in the previous section, it's valuable to take a step back after each of these refactors, and evaluate whether the end result is indeed simpler and easier to work with than what we had before it was refactored.

4.3 State as Entropy

Entropy can be defined as a lack of order or predictability. The more entropy there is in a system, the more disordered and unpredictable the system becomes. Program state is a lot like entropy. Whether we're discussing global application state, user session state, or a particular component instance's state for a given user session, each bit of state we introduce to an application creates a new dimension to take into account when trying to understand the flow of a program, how it came to the state it's currently at, or how the current state dictates and helps predict the flow moving forward.

In this section, we'll discuss ways of eliminating and containing state, as well as immutability. First off, let's discuss what constitutes current state.

4.3.1 Current State: It's Complicated

The problem with state is that, as an application grows, its state tree inevitably grows with it, and for this reason large applications are hopelessly complex. This complexity exists in the whole, but not necessarily in individual pieces. This is why breaking an application into ever smaller components might reduce local complexity even when it increases overall complexity. That is to say, breaking a single large function into a dozen small functions might make the overall application more complex, as there would be 10 times as many pieces. But it also makes the individual aspects of the previously large function that are now covered by each small function simpler when we're focused on them, as thus easier-to-maintain individual pieces of a large, complicated system, without requiring a complete or even vast understanding of the system as a whole.

At its heart, state is mutable. Even if the variable bindings themselves are immutable, the complete picture is mutable. A function might return a different object every time, and we may even make that object immutable so that the object itself doesn't change either, but anything that consumes the function receives a different object each time. Different objects mean different references, meaning the state as a whole mutates.

Consider a game of chess: each of two players starts with 16 pieces, each deterministically assigned a position on a checkerboard. The initial state is always the same. As each player inputs their actions, moving and trading pieces, the system state mutates. A few moves into the game, there is a good chance we'll be facing a game state we haven't ever experienced before. Computer program state is a lot like a game of chess, except there's more nuance in the way of user input, and an infinitude of possible board positions and state permutations.

In the world of web development, a human decides to open a new tab in their favorite web browser and then search Google for "cat in a pickle gifs." The browser allocates a new process through a system call to the operating system, which shifts some bits around on the physical hardware that lies inside the human's computer. Before the HTTP request hits the network, we need to hit DNS servers, engaging in the elaborate process of casting *google.com* into an IP address. The browser then checks whether a *ServiceWorker* is installed, and assuming there isn't one, the request finally takes the default route of querying Google's servers for the phrase "cat in a pickle gifs."

Naturally, Google receives this request at one of the frontend edges of its public network, in charge of balancing the load and routing requests to healthy backend services. The query goes through a variety of analyzers that attempt to break it down to its semantic roots, stripping the query down to its essential keywords to better match relevant results.

The search engine figures out the 10 most relevant results for "cat pickle gif" out of billions of pages in its index, which was of course primed by a different system that's also part of the whole. At the same time, Google pulls down a highly targeted piece of relevant advertisement about cat gifs that matches what it believes is the demographic the human making the query belongs to, thanks to a sophisticated ad network that figures out whether the user is authenticated with Google through an HTTP header session cookie. The search results page starts being constructed and streamed to the human, who now appears impatient and fidgety.

As the first few bits of HTML begin streaming down the wire, the search engine produces its result and hands it back to the frontend servers, which include it in the HTML stream that's sent back to the human. The web browser has been working hard at this too, parsing the incomplete pieces of HTML that have been streaming down the wire as best it could, even daring to launch other admirably and equally mind-boggling requests for HTTP resources presumed to be JavaScript, CSS, font, and image files as the HTML continues to stream down the wire. The first few chunks of HTML are converted into a DOM tree, and the browser would finally be able to begin rendering bits and pieces of the page on the screen, if it weren't for the pending, equally mind-boggling CSS and font requests.

As the CSS stylesheets and fonts are transmitted, the browser begins modeling the CSS Object Model (CSSOM) and getting a more complete picture of how to turn the HTML and CSS plain-text chunks provided by Google servers into a graphical representation that the human finds pleasant. Browser extensions get a chance to meddle with the content, removing the highly targeted piece of relevant advertisement about cat gifs before I even realize Google hoped I wouldn't block ads this time around.

A few seconds have passed since I first decided to search for cat in a pickle gifs. Needless to say, thousands of others brought similarly inane requests. To the same systems. During this time.

Not only does this example demonstrate the marvelous machinery and infrastructure that fuels even our most flippant daily computing experiences, but it also illustrates how abundantly hopeless it is to make sense of a system as a whole, let alone its comprehensive state at any given point in time. After all, where do we draw the boundaries? Within the code we wrote? The code that powers our customers' computers? Their hardware? The code that powers our servers? Its hardware? The internet as a whole? The power grid?

4.3.2 Eliminating Incidental State

We've established that the overall state of a system has little to do with our ability to comprehend parts of that same system. Our focus on reducing state-based entropy must then lie in the individual aspects of the system. It's for this reason that breaking apart large pieces of code is so effective. We're reducing the amount of state local to each given aspect of the system, and that's the kind of state that's worth taking care of, since it's what we can keep in our heads and make sense of.

Whenever persistence is involved, a discrepancy is going to exist between ephemeral state and realized state. In the case of a web application, we could define *ephemeral state* as any user input that hasn't resulted in state being persisted yet, as might be the case of an unsaved user preference that might be lost unless persisted. We can say *realized state* is the state that has been persisted, and that different programs might have different strategies on how to convert ephemeral state into realized state. A web application might adopt an offline-first pattern in which ephemeral state is automatically synchronized to an IndexedDB database in the browser, and eventually realized by updating the state persisted on a backend system. When the offline-first page is reloaded, unrealized state may be pushed to the backend or discarded.

Incidental state can occur when we have a piece of data that's used in several parts of an application, and that is derived from other pieces of data. When the original piece of data is updated, it wouldn't be hard to inadvertently leave the derived pieces of data in their current state, making them stale when compared to the updated original pieces of data. As an example, consider a piece of user input in Markdown and the HTML representation derived from that piece of Markdown. If the piece of Markdown is updated but the previously compiled pieces of HTML are not, then different parts of the system might display different bits of HTML out of what was apparently the same single Markdown source.

When we persist derived state, we're putting the original and the derived data at risk of falling out of sync. This isn't the case just when dealing with persistence layers, but can also occur in a few other scenarios as well. When dealing with caching layers, their content may become stale because the underlying original piece of content is updated but we forget to invalidate pieces of content derived from the updated data. Database denormalization is another common occurrence of this problem, whereby creating derived state can result in synchronization problems and stale byproducts of the original data.

This lack of synchronization is often observed in discussion forum software, as user profiles are denormalized into comment objects in an effort to save a database roundtrip. When users later update their profile, however, their old comments preserve a stale avatar, signature, or display name. To avoid this kind of issue, we should always consider recomputing derived state from its roots. Even though doing so won't always be possible, performant, or even practical, encouraging this kind of thinking across a development team will, if anything, increase awareness about the subtle intricacies of denormalized state.

As long as we're aware of the risks of data denormalization, we can then indulge in it. A parallel could be drawn to the case of performance optimization, as we should be aware that attempting to optimize a program based on microbenchmarks instead of data-driven optimization will most likely result in wasted developer time. Furthermore, just as with caches and other intermediate representations of data, performance optimization can lead to bugs and code that's ultimately harder to maintain. This is why neither should be embarked upon lightly, unless in a certain business case where performance is hurting the bottom line.

4.3.3 Containing State

State is inevitable. As we discussed in Section 4.3.1, "Current State: It's Complicated," on page 86, the full picture hardly affects our ability to maintain small parts of that state tree. In the local case—each of the interrelated but ultimately separate pieces of code we work with day to day—all that matters are the inputs we receive and the outputs we produce. That said, generating a large amount of output when we could instead emit a single piece of information is undesirable.

When all intermediate state is contained inside a component instead of being leaked to others, we're reducing the friction in interacting with our component or function. The more we condense state into its smallest possible representation for output purposes, the better contained our functions will become. Incidentally, we're making the interface easier to consume. Since there's less state to draw from, there are fewer ways of consuming that state. This reduces the number of possible use cases, but by favoring composability over serving every possible need, we're making each piece of functionality, when evaluated on its own, simpler.

One other case in which we may incidentally increase complexity occurs whenever we modify the property values of an input. This type of operation should be made extremely explicit, so as to not be confused, and avoided where possible. If we assume functions to be defined as the equation between the inputs we receive and the outputs we produce, the side effects are ill-advised. Mutations on the input within the body of a function are one example of side effects,

---

which can be a source of bugs and confusion, particularly due to the difficulty in tracking down the source for these mutations.

It is common to observe functions that modify an input parameter and then return that parameter. This is often the case with `Array#map` callbacks, where the developer wants to change a property or two on each object in a list, but also to preserve the original objects as the elements in the collection, as shown in the following example:

```
movies.map(movie => {
  movie.profit = movie.gross - movie.budget
  return movie
})
```

In these cases, it might be best to avoid using `Array#map` altogether, using `Array#forEach` or `for..of` instead, as shown here:

```
for (const movie of movies) {
  movie.profit = movie.gross - movie.budget
}
```

Neither `Array#forEach` nor `for..of` allow for chaining, assuming you wanted to filter the `movies` by criteria such as "profit is greater than $15M"; they're pure loops that don't produce any output. This is a good problem to have, however, because it explicitly separates data mutations at the `movie` item level, where we're adding a `profit` property to each item in `movies`, from transformations at the `movies` level, where we want to produce an entirely new collection consisting of only expensive movies:

```
for (const movie of movies) {
  movie.profit = movie.amount * movie.unitCost
}
const successfulMovies = movies.filter(
  movie => movie.profit > 15
)
```

Relying on immutability is an alternative that doesn't involve pure loops nor resort to breakage-prone side effects.

4.3.4 Leveraging Immutability

The following example takes advantage of the object spread operator to copy every property of `movie` into a new object, and then adds a `profit` property to it. Here we're creating a new collection, made up of new `movie` objects:

```
const movieModels = movies.map(movie => ({
  ...movie,
  profit: movie.amount * movie.unitCost
}))
const successfulMovies = movieModels.filter(
  movie => movie.profit > 15
)
```

Thanks to us making fresh copies of the objects we're working with, we've preserved the `movies` collection. If we assume at this point that `movies` was an input to our function, we could say that modifying any movie in that collection would've made our function impure, since it'd have the side effect of unexpectedly altering the input.

By introducing immutability, we've kept the function pure. That means that its output depends on only its inputs and that we don't create any side effects such as changing the inputs themselves. This, in turn, guarantees that the function is idempotent; calling a function repeatedly with the same input always produces the same result, given the output depends solely on the inputs and there are no side effects. In contrast, the idempotence property would've been brought into question if we had tainted the input by adding a `profit` field to every movie.

Large amounts of intermediate state or logic that permutates data into different shapes, back and forth, may be a signal that we've chosen poor representations of our data. When the right data structures are identified, we'll notice that a lot less transformation, mapping, and looping are involved in getting inputs to become the outputs we need to produce. In the next section we'll dive deeper into data structures.

4.4 Data Structures Are King

Data structures can make or break an application, as design decisions around data structures govern how those structures will be accessed. Consider the following piece of code, which provides a list of blog posts:

```
[{
  slug: 'understanding-javascript-async-await',
  title: 'Understanding JavaScript's async await',
  contents: '...'
}, {
  slug: 'pattern-matching-in-ecmascript',
  title: 'Pattern Matching in ECMAScript',
```

```
      contents: '...'
   }, ...]
```

An array-based list is great whenever we need to sort the list or map
its objects into a different representation, such as HTML. It's not so
great at other things, such as finding individual elements to use,
update, or remove. Arrays also make it harder to preserve unique-
ness, such as if we wanted to ensure that the slug field is unique
across all blog posts. In these cases, we could opt for an object-map-
based approach, as the one shown next:

```
{
   'understanding-javascript-async-await': {
      slug: 'understanding-javascript-async-await',
      title: 'Understanding JavaScript's async await',
      contents: '...'
   },
   'pattern-matching-in-ecmascript': {
      slug: 'pattern-matching-in-ecmascript',
      title: 'Pattern Matching in ECMAScript',
      contents: '...'
   },
   ...
}
```

Using Map, we could create a similar structure and benefit from the
native Map API as well:

```
new Map([
   ['understanding-javascript-async-await', {
      slug: 'understanding-javascript-async-await',
      title: 'Understanding JavaScript's async await',
      contents: '...'
   }],
   ['pattern-matching-in-ecmascript', {
      slug: 'pattern-matching-in-ecmascript',
      title: 'Pattern Matching in ECMAScript',
      contents: '...'
   }],
   ...
])
```

The data structure we select constrains and determines the shape
our API can take. Complex programs are often, in no small part, the
end result of combining poor data structures with new or unforeseen requirements that don't exactly fit in well with those structures.
It's usually well worth it to transform data into something that's
amenable to the task at hand so that the algorithm is simplified by
making the data easier to consume.

Now, we can't possibly foresee all scenarios when coming up with the data structure we'll use at first, but what we can do is create intermediate representations of the same underlying data by using new structures that do fit the new requirements. We can then leverage these structures, which were optimized for the new requirements, when writing code to fulfill those requirements. The alternative, resorting to the original data structure when writing new code that doesn't quite fit with it, will invariably result in logic that has to work around the limitations of the existing data structure, and as a result, we'll end up with less-than-ideal code, which might take some effort understanding and updating.

When we take the road of adapting data structures to the changing needs of our programs, we'll find that writing programs in such a data-driven way is better than relying on logic alone to drive their behaviors. When the data lends itself to the algorithms that work with it, our programs become straightforward: the logic focuses on the business problem being solved, while the data is focused on avoiding an interleaving of data transformations within the program logic itself. By making a hard separation between data or its representations and the logic that acts upon it, we're keeping different concerns separate. When we differentiate the two, data is data, and logic stays logic.

4.4.1 Isolating Data and Logic

Keeping data strictly separate from methods that modify or access those data structures can help reduce complexity. When data is not cluttered with functionality, it becomes detached from it and thus easier to read, understand, and serialize. At the same time, the logic that was previously tied to our data can now be used when accessing different bits of data that share some trait with it.

As an example, the following piece of code shows a piece of data that's encumbered by the logic that works with it. Whenever we want to leverage the methods of `Value`, we'll have to box our input in this class, and if we later want to unbox the output, we'll need to cast it with a custom-built `valueOf` method or similar:

```
class Value {
  constructor(value) {
    this.state = value
  }
  add(value) {
```

```
      this.state += value
      return this
   }
   multiply(value) {
      this.state *= value
      return this
   }
   valueOf() {
      return this.state
   }
}
console.log(+new Value(5).add(3).multiply(2)) // <- 16
```

Consider now, in contrast, the following piece of code. Here we have a couple of functions that purely compute addition and multiplication of their inputs, which are idempotent, and which can be used without boxing inputs into instances of Value, making the code more transparent to the reader. The idempotence aspect is of great benefit, because it makes the code more digestible: whenever we add 3 to 5, we know the output will be 8, whereas whenever we add 3 to the current state, we know only that Value will increment its state by 3:

```
function add(current, value) {
   return current + value
}
function multiply(current, value) {
   return current * value
}
console.log(multiply(add(5, 3), 2)) // <- 16
```

Taking this concept beyond basic mathematics, we can begin to see how this decoupling of form and function, or state and logic, can be increasingly beneficial. It's easier to serialize plain data over the wire, keep it consistent across different environments, and make it interoperable regardless of the logic, than if we tightly coupled data and the logic around it.

Functions are, to a certain degree, hopelessly coupled to the data they receive as inputs: in order for the function to work as expected, the data it receives must satisfy its contract for that piece of input. Within the bounds of a function's proper execution, the data must have a certain shape, traits, or adhere to whatever restrictions the function has in place. These restrictions may be somewhat lax (e.g., "must have a toString method"), highly specific (e.g., "must be a function that accepts three arguments and returns a decimal number between 0 and 1"), or anywhere in between. A simple interface is usually highly restrictive (e.g., accepting only a Boolean value). Meanwhile, it's common for loose interfaces to become burdened by their own flexibility, leading to complex implementations that attempt to accommodate many shapes and sizes of the same input parameter.

We should aim to keep logic restrictive and only as flexible as deemed necessary by business requirements. When an interface starts out being restrictive, we can always slowly open it up later as new use cases and requirements arise. By starting out with a small use case, we're able to grow the interface into something that's naturally better fit to handle specific, real-world use cases.

Data, on the other hand, should be transformed to fit elegant interfaces, rather than trying to fit the same data structure into every function. Doing so would result in frustration similar to that caused by a rushed abstraction layer that doesn't lend itself to being effortlessly consumed to leverage the implementations underlying it. These transformations should be kept separate from the data itself, so as to ensure reusability of each intermediate representation of the data on its own.

4.4.2 Restricting and Clustering Logic

Should a data structure—or code that leverages that data structure—require changes, the ripple effects can be devastating when the relevant logic is sprinkled all across the codebase. Consequently, when this happens, we need to update code from all over, making a point of not missing any occurrences, updating and fixing test cases as we go, and testing some more to certify that the updates haven't broken down our application logic, all in one fell swoop.

For this reason, we should strive to keep code that deals with a particular data structure contained in as few modules as possible. For instance, if we have a `BlogPost` database model, it probably makes sense to start out having all the logic regarding a `BlogPost` in a single file. In that file, we could expose an API allowing consumers to create, publish, edit, delete, update, search, or share blog posts. As the functionality around blog posts grows, we might opt for spreading the logic into multiple colocated files: one might deal with search, parsing raw end-user queries for tags and terms that are then passed to Elasticsearch or some other search engine; another might deal with sharing, exposing an API to share articles via email or through different social media platforms; and so on.

Splitting logic into a few files under the same directory helps us prevent an explosion of functionality that mostly just has a data structure in common, bringing together code that's closely related in terms of functionality.

The alternative, placing logic related to a particular aspect of our application such as blog posts directly in the components where it's needed, will cause trouble if left unchecked. Doing so might be beneficial in terms of short-term productivity, but longer-term we need to worry about coupling logic, strictly related to blog posts in this case, together with entirely different concerns. At the same time, if we sprinkle the bulk of the logic across several unrelated components, we risk missing critical aspects of functionality when making large-scale updates to the codebase. We might end up making the wrong assumptions, or mistakes that become evident only much further down the line.

It's acceptable to start out placing logic directly where it's needed at first, when it's unclear whether the functionality will grow or how much. Once this initial exploratory period elapses, and it becomes clear the functionality is here to stay and more might be to come, it's advisable that we isolate the functionality for the reasons stated previously. Later, as the functionality grows in size and in concerns that need to be addressed, we can componentize each aspect into different modules that are still grouped together logically in the filesystem, making it easy to take all of the interrelated concerns into account when need be.

Now that we have broken down the essentials of module design and how to delineate interfaces, as well as how to lock down, isolate, and drive down complexity in our internal implementations, we're ready to start discussing JavaScript-specific language features and an assortment of patterns that we can benefit from.

CHAPTER 5

Modular Patterns and Practices

In this chapter, we'll take a look at some of the latest language features and how to leverage those in our programs while reducing complexity in the process. We'll also analyze concrete coding patterns and conventions that can help us develop simple alternatives to otherwise complex problems.

5.1 Leveraging Modern JavaScript

When used judiciously, the latest JavaScript features can be of great help in reducing the amount of code whose sole purpose is to work around language limitations. This increases *signal*—the amount of valuable information that can be extracted from reading a piece of code—while eliminating boilerplate and repetition.

5.1.1 Template Literals

Before ES6, the JavaScript community came up with half a dozen ways of arriving at multiline strings: from strings chained with \ escape characters or + arithmetic operators, to using `Array#join`, or resorting to the string representation of comments in a function—all merely for multiline support.

Further, inserting variables into a string isn't possible, but that's easily circumvented by concatenating them with one or more strings:

```
'Hello ' + name + ', I\'m Nicolás!'
```

Template literals arrived in ES6 and resolve multiline strings in a feature that was native to the language, without the need for any clever hacks in user-space.

Unlike strings, with template literals, we can interpolate expressions by using a streamlined syntax. They involve less escaping, too, thanks to using backticks instead of single or double quotation marks, which appear more frequently in English text:

```
`Hello ${ name }, I'm Nicolás!`
```

Besides these improvements, template literals also offer the possibility of tagged templates. You can prefix the template with a custom function that transforms the template's output, enabling use cases like input sanitization, formatting, or anything else.

As an illustrative example, the following function could be used for the sanitization use case mentioned previously. Any expressions interpolated into a template go through the insane function from a library by the same name, which strips out unsafe bits of HTML—tags, attributes, or whole trees—to keep user-provided strings honest:

```
import insane from 'insane'

function sanitize(template, ...expressions) {
  return template.reduce((accumulator, part, i) => {
    return accumulator + insane(expressions[i - 1]) + part
  })
}
```

In the following example, we embed a user-provided comment as an interpolated expression in a template literal, and the sanitize tag takes care of the rest:

```
const comment = 'exploit time! <iframe src="http://evil.corp">
             </iframe>'
const html = sanitize`<div>${ comment }</div>`
console.log(html)
// <- '<div>exploit time! </div>'
```

Whenever we need to compose a string by using data, template literals are a terse alternative to string concatenation. When we want to avoid escaping single or double quotes, template literals can help. The same is true when we want to write multiline strings.

In every other case—when there's no interpolation, escaping, or multiline needs—the choice comes down to a mere matter of style.

In the last chapter of *Practical Modern JavaScript*, "Practical Considerations," I advocated in favor of using template literals in every case.[1] This was for a few reasons, but here are the two most important ones: because of convenience, so that you don't have to convert a string back and forth between single-quoted string and template literals depending on its contents; and because of consistency, so that you don't have to stop and think about which kind of quotation mark (single, double, or backtick) to use each time. Template literals may take some time to get accustomed to; we've used single-quoted strings for a long time, and template literals have been around only for a while. You or your team might prefer sticking with single-quoted strings, and that's perfectly fine too.

When it comes to style choices, you'll rarely face problems if you let your team come to a consensus about the preferred style choice and later enforce that choice by way of a lint tool like ESLint. It's entirely valid to stick with single-quoted strings and use template literals only when deemed absolutely necessary, if that's what most of the team prefers.

Using a tool like ESLint and a continuous integration job to enforce its rules means nobody has to perform the time-consuming job of keeping everyone in line with the house style. When tooling enforces style choices, discussions about those choices won't crop up as often in discussion threads while contributors are collaborating on units of work.

It's important to differentiate between purely stylistic choices, which tend to devolve into contentious time-sinking discussions, and choices that offer more ground to be covered in the everlasting battle against complexity. While the former may make a codebase subjectively easier to read, or more aesthetically pleasing, it is only through deliberate action that we keep complexity in check. Granted, a consistent style throughout a codebase can help contain

---

1 You can read a blog post I wrote about why template literals are better than strings at the Pony Foo site (*https://mjavascript.com/out/template-literals*). *Practical Modern JavaScript* (O'Reilly, 2017) is the first book in the Modular JavaScript series. You're currently reading the second book of that series.

complexity, but the exact style is unimportant as long as we enforce it consistently.

5.1.2 Destructuring, Rest, and Spread

The destructuring, rest, and spread features came into effect in ES6. These features accomplish various things, which we'll now discuss.

Destructuring helps us indicate the fields of an object that we'll be using to compute the output of a function. In the following example, we destructure a few properties from a `ticker` variable, and then combine that with a `...details` rest pattern containing every property of `ticker` that we haven't explicitly named in our destructuring pattern:

```
const { low, high, ask, ...details } = ticker
```

When we use destructuring methodically and near the top of our functions, or—even better—in the parameter list, we are making it obvious what the exact contract of our function is in terms of inputs.

Deep destructuring offers the ability to take this one step further, digging as deep as necessary into the structure of the object we're accessing. Consider the following example, where we destructure the JSON response body with details about an apartment. When we have a destructuring statement like this near the top of a function that's used to render a view, the aspects of the apartment listing that are needed to render it become self-evident at a glance. In addition, we avoid repetition when accessing property chains like `response.contact.name` or `response.contact.phone`:

```
const {
  title,
  description,
  askingPrice,
  features: {
    area,
    bathrooms,
    bedrooms,
    amenities
  },
  contact: {
    name,
    phone,
    email
  }
} = response
```

At times, a deeply destructured property name may not make sense outside its context. For instance, we introduce `name` to our scope, but it's the name of the contact for the listing, not to be confused with the name of the listing itself. We can clarify this by giving the contact's `name` an alias, like `contactName` or `responseContactName`:

```
const {
  title,
  description,
  askingPrice,
  features: {
    area,
    bathrooms,
    bedrooms,
    amenities
  },
  contact: {
    name: responseContactName,
    phone,
    email
  }
} = response
```

When using `:` to alias, it can be difficult at first to remember whether the original name or the aliased name comes first. One helpful way to keep it straight is to mentally replace `:` with the word "as." That way, `name: responseContactName` would read as "name as responseContactName."

We can even have the same property listed twice, if we wanted to destructure some of its contents, while also maintaining access to the object itself. For instance, if we wanted to destructure the contact object's contents, as we do in the preceding example, but also take a reference to the whole `contact` object, we can do the following:

```
const {
  title,
  description,
  askingPrice,
  features: {
    area,
    bathrooms,
    bedrooms,
    amenities
  },
  contact: responseContact,
  contact: {
```

```
    name: responseContactName,
    phone,
    email
  }
} = response
```

Object spread helps us create a shallow copy of an object by using a little native syntax. We can also combine object spread with our own properties, so that we create a copy that also overwrites the values in the original object we're spreading:

```
const faxCopy = { ...fax }
const newCopy = { ...fax, date: new Date() }
```

This allows us to create slightly modified shallow copies of other objects. When dealing with discrete state management, this means we don't need to resort to `Object.assign` method calls or utility libraries. While there's nothing inherently wrong with `Object.assign` calls, the object spread ... abstraction is easier for us to internalize and mentally map its meaning back to `Object.assign` without us realizing it, and so the code becomes easier to read because we're dealing with less unabstracted knowledge.

Another benefit worth pointing out is that `Object.assign()` can cause accidents: if we forget to pass an empty object literal as the first argument for this use case, we end up mutating the object. With object spread, there is no way to accidentally mutate anything, since the pattern always acts as if an empty object was passed to `Object.assign` in the first position.

5.1.3 Striving for Simple const Bindings

If we use `const` by default, the need to use `let` or `var` can be ascribed to code that's more complicated than it should be. Striving to avoid those kinds of bindings almost always leads to better and simpler code.

In Section 4.2.4, "Extracting Functions," on page 76 we saw a `let` binding that was assigned a default value and had conditional statements immediately after that might change the contents of the variable binding:

```
// ...
let type = 'contributor'
if (user.administrator) {
  type = 'administrator'
} else if (user.roles.includes('edit_articles')) {
```

```
  type = 'editor'
}
// ...
```

Most reasons that we may need to use `let` or `var` bindings are variants of the preceding example and can be resolved by extracting the assignments into a function where the returned value is then assigned to a `const` binding. This moves the complexity out of the way, and eliminates the need for looking ahead to see whether the binding is reassigned at some point in the code flow later:

```
// ...
const type = getUserType(user)
// ...

function getUserType(user) {
  if (user.administrator) {
    return 'administrator'
  }
  if (user.roles.includes('edit_articles')) {
    return 'editor'
  }
  return 'contributor'
}
```

A variant of this problem occurs when we repeatedly assign the result of an operation to the same binding, in order to split it into several lines:

```
let values = [1, 2, 3, 4, 5]
values = values.map(value => value * 2)
values = values.filter(value => value > 5)
// <- [6, 8, 10]
```

An alternative is to avoid reassignment, and instead use chaining:

```
const finalValues = [1, 2, 3, 4, 5]
  .map(value => value * 2)
  .filter(value => value > 5)
// <- [6, 8, 10]
```

A better approach is to create new bindings every time, computing their values based on the previous binding, and picking up the benefits of using `const` in doing so. We can then rest assured that the binding doesn't change later in the flow:

```
const initialValues = [1, 2, 3, 4, 5]
const doubledValues = initialValues.map(value => value * 2)
const finalValues = doubledValues.filter(value => value > 5)
// <- [6, 8, 10]
```

Let's move onto a more interesting topic: asynchronous code flows.

5.1.4 Navigating Callbacks, Promises, and Asynchronous Functions

JavaScript now offers several options when it comes to describing asynchronous algorithms: the plain callback pattern, promises, async functions, async iterators, async generators, plus any patterns offered by libraries consumed in our applications.

Each solution comes with its own set of strengths and weaknesses:

- Callbacks are typically a solid choice, but we often need to involve libraries when we want to execute our work concurrently.

- Promises might be hard to understand at first, but they offer a few utilities like `Promise#all` for concurrent work, yet they might be hard to debug under some circumstances.

- Async functions require a bit of understanding on top of being comfortable with promises, but they're easier to debug and often result in simpler code, plus they can be interspersed with synchronous functions rather easily as well.

- Iterators and generators are powerful tools, but they don't have all that many practical use cases, so we must consider whether we're using them because they fit our needs or just because we can.

It could be argued that callbacks are the simplest mechanism, although a similar case could be made for promises now that so much of the language is built around them. In any case, consistency should remain the primary driving force behind deciding which pattern to use. While it's okay to mix and match a few different patterns, most of the time we should be using the same patterns again and again, so that our team can develop a sense of familiarity with the codebase, instead of having to guess whenever encountering an unchartered portion of the application.

Using promises and async functions inevitably involves casting callbacks into this pattern. In the following example, we make up a `delay` function that returns promises that settle after a provided timeout:

```
function delay(timeout) {
  const resolver = resolve => {
    setTimeout(() => {
      resolve()
    }, timeout)
  }
  return new Promise(resolver)
}
delay(2000).then(...)
```

A similar pattern would have to be used to consume functions taking a last argument that's an error-first callback-style function in Node.js. Starting with Node.js v8.0.0, however, a built-in utility "promisifies" these callback-based functions so that they return promises:[2]

```
import { promisify } from 'util'
import { readFile } from 'fs'
const readFilePromise = promisify(readFile)

readFilePromise('./data.json', 'utf8').then(data => {
  console.log(`Data: ${ data }`)
})
```

Libraries could do the same for the client-side (one example is blue bird) or we can create our own promisify. In essence, promisify takes the function that we want to use in promise-based flows, and returns a different, "promisified" function that returns a promise where we call our function passing all the provided arguments plus a custom callback, which settles the promise after deciding whether it should be fulfilled or rejected:

```
// promisify.js
export default function promisify(fn) {
  return (...rest) => {
    return new Promise((resolve, reject) => {
      fn(...rest, (err, result) => {
        if (err) {
          reject(err)
          return
        }
        resolve(result)
      })
    })
  }
}
```

---

2 Note also that, starting in Node.js v10.0.0, the native `fs.promises` interface can be used to access promise-based versions of the `fs` module's methods.

```
    }
  }
```

Using a `promisify` function, then, would be no different from the earlier example with `readFile`, except we'd be providing our own `promisify` implementation:

```
import promisify from './promisify'
import { readFile } from 'fs'
const readFilePromise = promisify(readFile)

readFilePromise('./data.json', 'utf8').then(data => {
  console.log(`Data: ${ data }`)
})
```

Casting promises back into a callback-based format is less involved because we can add reactions to handle both the fulfillment and rejection results, and call back `done`, passing in the corresponding result where appropriate:

```
function unpromisify(p, done) {
  p.then(
    data => done(null, data),
    error => done(error)
  )
}
unpromisify(delay(2000), err => {
  // ...
})
```

Lastly, when it comes to converting promises to async functions, the language acts as a native compatibility layer, boxing every expression we `await` on into promises, so there's no need for any casting at the application level.

We can apply our guidelines for clear code to asynchronous code flows as well, because no fundamental differences are at play in the way we write these functions. Our focus should be on how these flows are connected together, regardless of whether they're composed of callbacks, promises, or something else. When plumbing tasks together, one of the main sources of complexity is nesting. When several tasks are nested in a tree-like shape, we might end up with code that's deeply nested. One of the best solutions to this readability problem is to break our flow into smaller trees, which would consequently be more shallow. We'll have to connect these trees together by adding a few extra function calls, but we'll have removed significant complexity when trying to understand the general flow of operations.

5.2 Composition and Inheritance

Let's explore how to improve our application designs beyond what JavaScript offers purely at the language level. In this section, we'll discuss two approaches to growing parts of a codebase:

Inheritance
> We scale vertically by stacking pieces of code on top of each other so that we can leverage existing features while customizing others and adding our own.

Composition
> We scale our application horizontally by adding related or unrelated pieces of code at the same level of abstraction while keeping complexity to a minimum.

5.2.1 Inheritance Through Classes

Until ES6 introduced first-class syntax for prototypal inheritance to JavaScript, prototypes weren't a widely used feature in user-land. Instead, libraries offered helper methods that made inheritance simpler, using prototypal inheritance under the hood, but hiding the implementation details from their consumers. Even though ES6 classes look a lot like classes in other languages, they're syntactic sugar, using prototypes under the hood and making them compatible with older techniques and libraries.

Through the introduction of a `class` keyword, paired with the React framework originally hailing classes as the go-to way of declaring stateful components, classes have helped spark some love for a pattern that was previously quite unpopular when it comes to JavaScript. In the case of React, the base `Component` class offers lightweight state management methods, while leaving the rendering and lifecycle up to the consumer classes extending `Component`. When necessary, the consumer can also decide to implement methods such as `componentDidMount`, which allows for event binding after a component tree is mounted; `componentDidCatch`, which can be used to trap unhandled exceptions that arise during the component lifecycle; among a variety of other soft interface methods. There's no mention of these optional lifecycle hooks anywhere in the base `Component` class, which are instead confined to the rendering mechanisms of React. In this sense, we note that the `Component` class stays focused on state management, while everything else is offered up by the consumer.

Inheritance is also useful when there's an abstract interface to implement and methods to override, particularly when the objects being represented can be mapped to the real world. In practical terms and in the case of JavaScript, inheritance works great when the prototype being extended offers a good description for the parent prototype: a `Car` is a `Vehicle`, but a car is not a `SteeringWheel`; the wheel is just one aspect of the car.

5.2.2 The Perks of Composition: Aspects and Extensions

With inheritance, we can add layers of complexity to an object. These layers are meant to be ordered: we start with the least specific foundational bits of the object and build our way up to the most specific aspects of it. When we write code based on inheritance chains, complexity is spread across the different classes, but lies mostly at the foundational layers that offer a terse API while hiding this complexity away.

Composition is an alternative to inheritance. Rather than building objects by vertically stacking functionality, composition relies on stringing together orthogonal aspects of functionality. In this sense, *orthogonality* means that the bits of functionality we compose complement, but do not alter the behavior of, each other.

One way to compose functionality is additive: we could write extension functions, which augment existing objects with new functionality. In the following code snippet, a `makeEmitter` function adds flexible event-handling functionality to any target object, providing it with an `.on` method, where we can add event listeners to the target object; and an `.emit` method, where the consumer can indicate a type of event and any number of parameters to be passed to event listeners:

```
function makeEmitter(target) {
  const listeners = []

  target.on = (eventType, listener) => {
    if (!(eventType in listeners)) {
      listeners[eventType] = []
    }

    listeners[eventType].push(listener)
```

```
  }

  target.emit = (eventType, ...params) => {
    if (!(eventType in listeners)) {
      return
    }

    listeners[eventType].forEach(listener => {
      listener(...params)
    })
  }

  return target
}

const person = makeEmitter({
  name: 'Artemisa',
  age: 27
})

person.on('move', (x, y) => {
  console.log(`${ person.name } moved to [${ x }, ${ y }].`)
})

person.emit('move', 23, 5)
// <- 'Artemisa moved to [23, 5].'
```

This approach is versatile, helping us add event emission functionality to any object without the need to add an `EventEmitter` class somewhere in the prototype chain of the object. This is useful when you don't own the base class, when the targets aren't class-based, or when the functionality to be added isn't meant to be part of every instance of a class; there are persons who emit events and persons who are quiet and don't need this functionality.

Another way of doing composition, which doesn't rely on extension functions, is to rely on functional aspects instead, without mutating your target object. In the following snippet, we do just that: we have an `emitters` map that stores target objects and maps them to the event listeners they have, an `onEvent` function that associates event listeners to target objects, and an `emitEvent` function that fires all event listeners of a given type for a target object, passing the provided parameters. All of this is accomplished in such a way that there's no need to modify the `person` object in order to have event-handling capabilities associated with the object:

```
const emitters = new WeakMap()

function onEvent(target, eventType, listener) {
  if (!emitters.has(target)) {
    emitters.set(target, new Map())
  }

  const listeners = emitters.get(target)

  if (!(eventType in listeners)) {
    listeners.set(eventType, [])
  }

  listeners.get(eventType).push(listener)
}

function emitEvent(target, eventType, ...params) {
  if (!emitters.has(target)) {
    return
  }

  const listeners = emitters.get(target)

  if (!listeners.has(eventType)) {
    return
  }

  listeners.get(eventType).forEach(listener => {
    listener(...params)
  })
}

const person = {
  name: 'Artemisa',
  age: 27
}

onEvent(person, 'move', (x, y) => {
  console.log(`${ person.name } moved to [${ x }, ${ y }].`)
})

emitEvent(person, 'move', 23, 5)
// <- 'Artemisa moved to [23, 5].'
```

Note that we're using both WeakMap and Map here. Using a plain Map would prevent garbage collection from cleaning things up when target is being referenced only by Map entries, whereas WeakMap allows garbage collection to take place on the objects that make up its keys. Given that we usually want to attach events to objects, we can use WeakMap as a way to avoid creating strong references that might end up causing memory leaks. On the other hand, it's okay to use a regular `Map` for the event listeners, given those are associated to an event-type string.

Let's move on to deciding whether to use inheritance, extension functions, or functional composition. We'll see where each pattern shines, and when to avoid them.

5.2.3 Choosing Between Composition and Inheritance

In the real world, you'll seldom have to use inheritance except when connecting to specific frameworks you depend on, to apply specific patterns such as extending native JavaScript arrays, or when performance is of the utmost necessity. When it comes to performance as a reason for using prototypes, we should highlight the need to test our assumptions and measure different approaches before jumping all in to a pattern that might not be ideal to work with, for the sake of a performance gain we might not observe.

Decoration and functional composition are friendlier patterns because they aren't as restrictive. Once you inherit from something, you can't later choose to inherit from something else, unless you keep adding inheritance layers to your prototype chain. This becomes a problem when several classes inherit from a base class but then need to branch out while still sharing different portions of functionality. In these cases and many others, using composition is going to let us pick and choose the functionality we need without sacrificing our flexibility.

The functional approach is a bit more cumbersome to implement than simply mutating objects or adding base classes, but it offers the most flexibility. By avoiding changes to the underlying target, we keep objects easy to serialize into JSON, unencumbered by a growing collection of methods, and thus more readily compatible across our codebase.

Furthermore, using base classes makes it a bit hard to reuse the logic at varying insertion points in our prototype chains. Using extension functions, likewise, makes it challenging to add similar methods that support slightly different use cases. Using a functional approach leads to less coupling in this regard, but it could also complicate the underlying implementation of the makeup for objects, making it hard to decipher how their functionality ties in together, tainting our fundamental understanding of the way code flows and making debugging sessions longer than need be.

As with most things programming, your codebase benefits from a semblance of consistency. Even if you use all three patterns, (and others), a codebase that uses half a dozen patterns in equal amounts is harder to understand, work with, and build on, than an equivalent codebase that instead uses one pattern for the vast majority of its code while using other patterns in smaller ways when warranted. Choosing the right pattern for each situation and striving for consistency might seem at odds with each other, but this is again a balancing act. The trade-off is between consistency in the grand scale of our codebase versus simplicity in the local piece of code we're working on. The question to ask is then: are we obtaining enough of a simplicity gain that it warrants the sacrifice of some consistency?

5.3 Code Patterns

Digging a bit deeper and into more-specific elements of architecture design, in this section we'll explore a few of the most common patterns for creating boundaries from which complexity cannot escape, encapsulating functionality, and communicating across these boundaries or application layers.

5.3.1 Revealing Module

The revealing module pattern has become a staple in the world of JavaScript. The premise is simple enough: expose precisely what consumers should be able to access, and avoid exposing anything else. The reasons for this are manifold. Preventing unwarranted access to implementation details reduces the likelihood of your module's interface being abused for unsupported use cases that might bring headaches to both the module implementor and the consumer alike.

Explicitly avoid exposing methods that are meant to be private, such as a hypothetical _calculatePriceHistory method, which relies on the leading underscore as a way of discouraging direct access and signaling that it should be regarded as private. Avoiding such methods prevents test code from accessing private methods directly, resulting in tests that make assertions solely regarding the interface and that can be later referenced as documentation on how to use the interface. This approach also prevents consumers from monkey-patching implementation details, leading to more transparent interfaces. Finally, this approach also often results in cleaner interfaces because the interface is all there is, and there are no alternative ways of interacting with the module through direct use of its internals.

JavaScript modules are of a revealing nature by default, making it easy for us to follow the revealing pattern of not giving away access to implementation details. Functions, objects, classes, and any other bindings we declare are private unless we explicitly decide to export them from the module.

When we expose only a thin interface, our implementation can change largely without having an impact on how consumers use the module, nor on the tests that cover the module. As a mental exercise, always be on the lookout for aspects of an interface that should be turned into implementation details and extricated from the interface itself.

5.3.2 Object Factories

Even when using JavaScript modules and strictly following the revealing pattern, we might end up with unintentional sharing of state across our usage of a module. Incidental state might result in unexpected results from an interface: consumers don't have a complete picture because other consumers are contributing changes to this shared state as well, sometimes making it hard to figure out what exactly is going on in an application.

If we were to move our functional event emitter code snippet, with onEvent and emitEvent, into a JavaScript module, we'd notice that the emitters map is now a lexical top-level binding for that module, meaning all of the module's scope has access to emitters. This is what we'd want, because that way, we can register event listeners in onEvent and fire them off in emitEvent. In most other situations, however, sharing persistent state across public interface methods is a recipe for unexpected bugs.

Suppose we have a calculator module that can be used to make basic calculations through a stream of operations. Even if consumers were supposed to use that model synchronously and flush state in one fell swoop, without allowing a second consumer to taint the state and produce unexpected results, our module shouldn't rely on consumer behavior to provide consistent results. The following contrived implementation relies on local shared state and would need consumers to use the module strictly as intended, making any calls to add and multiply, and leaving calculate as the last method that's meant to be called only once:

```
const operations = []
let state = 0

export function add(value) {
  operations.push(() => {
    state += value
  })
}

export function multiply(value) {
  operations.push(() => {
    state *= value
  })
}

export function calculate() {
  operations.forEach(op => op())
  return state
}
```

Here's an example of how consuming the previous module could work:

```
import { add, multiply, calculate } from './calculator'
add(3)
add(4)
multiply(-2)
calculate() // <- -14
```

As soon as we try to append operations in two places, things start getting out of hand, with the operations array getting bits and pieces of unrelated computations, tainting our calculations:

```
// a.js
import { add, calculate } from './calculator'
add(3)
setTimeout(() => {
  add(4)
  calculate() // <- 14, an extra 7 because of b.js
}, 100)

// b.js
import { add, calculate } from './calculator'
add(2)
calculate() // <- 5, an extra 3 from a.js
```

A slightly better approach gets rid of the `state` variable, and instead passes the state around operation handlers, so that each operation knows the current state and applies any necessary changes to it. The `calculate` step creates a new initial state each time, and goes from there:

```
const operations = []

export function add(value) {
  operations.push(state => state + value)
}

export function multiply(value) {
  operations.push(state => state * value)
}

export function calculate() {
  return operations.reduce((result, op) =>
    op(result)
  , 0)
}
```

This approach presents problems too, however. Even though the `state` is always reset to 0, we're treating unrelated operations as if they were all part of a whole, which is still wrong:

```
// a.js
import { add, calculate } from './calculator'
add(3)
setTimeout(() => {
  add(4)
  calculate() // <- 9, an extra 2 from b.js
}, 100)

// b.js
import { add, calculate } from './calculator'
add(2)
calculate() // <- 5, an extra 3 from a.js
```

Blatantly, our contrived module is poorly designed, as its operations buffer should never be used to drive several unrelated calculations. We should instead expose a factory function that returns an object from its own self-contained scope, where all relevant state is shut off from the outside world. The methods on this object are equivalent to the exported interface of a plain JavaScript module, but state mutations are contained to instances that consumers create:

```
export function getCalculator() {
  const operations = []
```

```
function add(value) {
  operations.push(state => state + value)
}

function multiply(value) {
  operations.push(state => state * value)
}

function calculate() {
  return operations.reduce((result, op) =>
    op(result)
  , 0)
}

return { add, multiply, calculate }
}
```

Using the calculator like this is just as straightforward, except that now we can do things asynchronously. Even if other consumers are also making computations of their own, each user will have their own state, preventing data corruption:

```
import { getCalculator } from './calculator'
const { add, multiply, calculate } = getCalculator()
add(3)
add(4)
multiply(-2)
calculate() // <- -14
```

Even with our two-file example, we wouldn't have any problems anymore, since each file would have its own atomic calculator:

```
// a.js
import { getCalculator } from './calculator'
const { add, calculate } = getCalculator()
add(3)
setTimeout(() => {
  add(4)
  calculate() // <- 7
}, 100)

// b.js
import { getCalculator } from './calculator'
const { add, calculate } = getCalculator()
add(2)
calculate() // <- 2
```

As we just showed, even when using modern language constructs and JavaScript modules, it's not too hard to create complications through shared state. Thus, we should always strive to contain mutable state as close to its consumers as possible.

5.3.3 Event Emission

We've already explored at length the pattern of registering event listeners associated to arbitrary plain JavaScript objects and firing events of any kind, triggering those listeners. Event handling is most useful when we want to have clearly delineated side effects.

In the browser, for instance, we can bind a `click` event to a specific DOM element. When the `click` event fires, we might issue an HTTP request, render a different page, start an animation, or play an audio file.

Events are a useful way of reporting progress whenever we're dealing with a queue. While processing a queue, we could fire a `progress` event whenever an item is processed, allowing the UI or any other consumer to render and update a progress indicator or apply a partial unit of work relying on the data processed by the queue.

Events also offer a mechanism to provide hooks into the lifecycle of an object. For example, the AngularJS view-rendering framework used event propagation to enable hierarchical communication across separate components. This allowed AngularJS codebases to keep components decoupled from one another while still being able to react to each other's state changes and interact.

Having event listeners allowed a component to receive a message, perhaps process it by updating its display elements, and then maybe reply with an event of its own, allowing for rich interaction without necessarily having to introduce another module to act as an intermediary.

5.3.4 Message Passing and the Simplicity of JSON

When it comes to `ServiceWorker`, web workers, browser extensions, frames, API calls, or WebSocket integrations, we might run into issues if we don't plan for robust data serialization ahead of time. This is a place where using classes to represent data can break down, because we need a way to serialize class instances into raw data (typically JSON) before sending it over the wire, and, crucially, the recipient needs to decode this JSON back into a class instance. It's the second part where classes start to fail since there isn't a

standardized way of reconstructing a class instance from JSON. For
example:

```
class Person {
  constructor(name, address) {
    this.name = name
    this.address = address
  }
  greet() {
    console.log(`Hi! My name is ${ this.name }.`)
  }
}

const rwanda = new Person('Rwanda', '123 Main St')
```

Although we can easily serialize our `rwanda` instance with
`JSON.stringify(rwanda)`, and then send it over the wire, the code
on the other end has no standard way of turning this JSON back
into an instance of our `Person` class, which might have a lot more
functionality than merely a `greet` function. The receiving end might
have no business deserializing this data back into the class instance
it originated from, but in some cases, there's merit to having an exact
replica object back on the other end. For example, to reduce friction
when passing messages between a website and a web worker, both
sides should be dealing in the same data structure. In such scenarios,
simple JavaScript objects are ideal.

JSON—now a subset of the JavaScript grammar—was purpose-built
for this use case, where we often have to serialize data, send it over
the wire, and deserialize it on the other end.[3] Plain JavaScript objects
are a great way to store data in our applications, offer frictionless
serialization out the box, and lead to cleaner data structures because
we can keep logic decoupled from the data.

When the language on both the sending and receiving ends is Java-
Script, we can share a module with all the functionality that we need
around the data structure. This way, we don't have to worry about
serialization, since we're using plain JavaScript objects and can rely
on JSON for the transport layer. We don't have to concern ourselves

---

3 Up until recently, JSON wasn't, strictly speaking, a proper subset of ECMA-262. A
  recent proposal (*https://mjavascript.com/out/json-subset*) has amended the ECMAScript
  specification to consider bits of JSON that were previously invalid JavaScript to be valid
  JavaScript.

with sharing functionality either, because we can rely on the Java-Script module system for that part.

Armed with a foundation for writing solid modules based on your own reasoning, we now turn the page to operational concerns such as handling application secrets responsibly, making sure our dependencies don't fail us, taking care of how we orchestrate build processes and continuous integration, and dealing with nuance in state management and the high-stakes decision-making around producing the right abstractions.

CHAPTER 6

Development Methodology and Philosophy

Even though most of us work on projects with source code that is not publicly available, we can all benefit from following open source best practices, many of which still apply in closed-source project development. Pretending all of our code is going to be open source results in better configuration and secret management, better documentation, better interfaces, and more maintainable codebases overall.

In this chapter, we'll explore open source principles and look at ways to adapt a methodology and set of robustness principles known as The Twelve-Factor App (generally devised for backend development) to modern JavaScript application development, frontend and backend alike.[1]

6.1 Secure Configuration Management

When it comes to configuration secrets in closed-source projects, like API keys or HTTPS session decryption keys, it is common for them to be hardcoded in place. In open source projects, these are typically instead obtained through environment variables or

---

1 You can find the original Twelve-Factor App methodology (*https://mjavascript.com/out/12factor*) and its documentation online.

encrypted configuration files that aren't committed to version-control systems alongside our codebase.

In open source projects, this allows the developer to share the vast majority of their application without compromising the security of their production systems. While this might not be an immediate concern in closed-source environments, we need to consider that once a secret is committed to version control, it's etched into our version history unless we force a rewrite of that history, scrubbing the secrets from existence. Even then, it cannot be guaranteed that a malicious actor hasn't gained access to these secrets at some point before they were scrubbed from history. Therefore, a better solution to this problem is rotating the secrets that might be compromised, revoking access through the old secrets and starting to use new, uncompromised secrets.

Although this approach is effective, it can be time-consuming when we have several secrets under our belt. When our application is large enough, leaked secrets pose significant risk even when exposed for a short period of time. As such, it's best to approach secrets with careful consideration by default, and avoid headaches later in the lifetime of a project.

The absolute least we could be doing is giving every secret a unique name and placing them in a JSON file. Any sensitive information or configurable values may qualify as a secret, and this might range from private signing keys used to sign certificates to port numbers or database connection strings:

```
{
  "PORT": 3000,
  "MONGO_URI": "mongodb://localhost/mjavascript",
  "SESSION_SECRET": "ditch-foot-husband-conqueror"
}
```

Instead of hardcoding these variables wherever they're used, or even placing them in a constant at the beginning of the module, we centralize all sensitive information in a single file that can then be excluded from version control. Besides helping us share the secrets across modules, making updates easier, this approach encourages us to isolate information that we previously wouldn't have considered sensitive, like the work factor used for salting passwords.

Another benefit of going down this road is that, because we have all environment configuration in a central store, we can point our application to a different secret store depending on whether we're provisioning the application for production, staging, or one of the local development environments used by our developers.

Because we're purposely excluding the secrets from source version control, we can take many approaches when sharing them, such as using environment variables, storing them in JSON files kept in an Amazon S3 bucket, or using an encrypted repository dedicated to our application secrets.

Using what's commonly referred to as *dot env* files is an effective way of securely managing secrets in Node.js applications, and a module called nconf can aid us in setting these up. These files typically contain two types of data: secrets that mustn't be shared outside execution environments, and configuration values that should be editable and that we don't want to hardcode.

One concrete and effective way of accomplishing this in real-world environments is using several *dot env* files, each with a clearly defined purpose. In order of precedence:

- *.env.defaults.json* can be used to define default values that aren't necessarily overwritten across environments, such as the application listening port, the NODE_ENV variable, and configurable options you don't want to hardcode into your application code. These default settings should be safe to check into source control.

- *.env.production.json*, *.env.staging.json*, and others can be used for environment-specific settings, such as the various production connection strings for databases, cookie encoding secrets, API keys, and so on.

- *.env.json* could be your local, machine-specific settings, useful for secrets or configuration changes that shouldn't be shared with other team members.

Furthermore, you could also accept simple modifications to environment settings through environment variables, such as when executing PORT=3000 node app, which is convenient during development.

We can use the nconf npm package to handle reading and merging all of these sources of application settings with ease.

The following piece of code shows how you could configure nconf to do what we've just described: we import the nconf package, and declare configuration sources from highest priority to lowest priority, while nconf will do the merging (higher-priority settings will always take precedence). We then set the actual NODE_ENV environment variable, because libraries rely on this property to decide whether to instrument or optimize their output:

```
// env
import nconf from 'nconf'

nconf.env()
nconf.file('environment', `.env.${ nodeEnv() }.json`)
nconf.file('machine', '.env.json')
nconf.file('defaults', '.env.defaults.json')

process.env.NODE_ENV = nodeEnv() // consistency

function nodeEnv() {
  return accessor('NODE_ENV')
}

function accessor(key) {
  return nconf.get(key)
}

export default accessor
```

The module also exposes an interface through which we can consume these application settings by making a function call such as env('PORT'). Whenever we need to access one of the configuration settings, we can import *env.js* and ask for the computed value of the relevant setting, and nconf takes care of the bulk of figuring out which settings take precedence over what, and what the value should be for the current environment:

```
import env from './env'

const port = env('PORT')
```

Assuming we have an *.env.defaults.json* that looks like the following, we could pass in the NODE_ENV flag when starting our staging, test, or production application and get the proper environment settings back, helping us simplify the process of loading up an environment:

```
{
  "NODE_ENV": "development"
}
```

We usually find ourselves needing to replicate this sort of logic in the client side. Naturally, we can't share server-side secrets in the client side, as that'd leak our secrets to anyone snooping through our JavaScript files in the browser. Still, we might want to be able to access a few environment settings such as the NODE_ENV, our application's domain or port, Google Analytics tracking ID, and similarly safe-to-advertise configuration details.

When it comes to the browser, we could use the exact same files and environment variables, but include a dedicated browser-specific object field, like so:

```
{
  "NODE_ENV": "development",
  "BROWSER_ENV": {
    "MIXPANEL_API_KEY": "some-api-key",
    "GOOGLE_MAPS_API_KEY": "another-api-key"
  }
}
```

Then, we could write a tiny script like the following to print all of those settings:

```
// print-browser-env
import env from './env'
const browserEnv = env('BROWSER_ENV')
const prettyJson = JSON.stringify(browserEnv, null, 2)
console.log(prettyJson)
```

Naturally, we don't want to mix server-side settings with browser settings. Browser settings are usually accessible to anyone with a user agent, the ability to visit our website, and basic programming skills, meaning we would do well not to bundle highly sensitive secrets with our client-side applications. To resolve the issue, we can have a build step that prints the settings for the appropriate environment to an *.env.browser.json* file, and then use only that file on the client-side.

We could incorporate this encapsulation into our build process, adding the following command-line call:

```
node print-browser-env > browser/.env.browser.json
```

Note that in order for this pattern to work properly, we need to know the environment we're building for at the time that we compile the browser dot env file. Passing in a different NODE_ENV environment variable would produce different results, depending on our target environment.

By compiling client-side configuration settings in this way, we avoid leaking server-side configuration secrets onto the client-side.

Furthermore, we should replicate the *env* file from the server side to the client side, so that application settings are consumed in much the same way on both sides of the wire:

```
// browser/env
import env from './env.browser.json'

export default function accessor(key) {
  if (typeof key !== 'string') {
    return env
  }
  return key in env ? env[key] : null
}
```

There are many other ways of storing our application settings, each with its own associated pros and cons. The approach we just discussed, though, is relatively easy to implement and solid enough to get started. As an upgrade, you might want to look into using AWS Secrets Manager. That way, you'd have a single secret to take care of in team members' environments, instead of every single secret.

A secret service also takes care of encryption, secure storage, and secret rotation (useful in the case of a data breach), among other advanced features.

6.2 Explicit Dependency Management

The reason that we sometimes feel tempted to check our dependencies into source control is so we get the exact same versions across the dependency tree, every time, in every environment.

Including dependency trees in our repositories is not practical, however, given these are typically in the hundreds of megabytes and frequently include compiled assets that are built based on the target environment and operating system.[2] The build process itself is environment-dependent, and thus not suitable for a presumably platform-agnostic code repository.

---

2 When we run npm install, npm also executes a rebuild step after npm install ends. The rebuild step recompiles native binaries, building different assets depending on the execution environment and the local machine's operating system.

During development, we want to make sure we get nonbreaking upgrades to our dependencies, which can help us resolve upstream bugs, tighten our grip around security vulnerabilities, and leverage new features or improvements. For deployments however, we want reproducible builds, where installing our dependencies yields the same results every time.

The solution is to include a dependency manifest, indicating the exact versions of the libraries in our dependency tree that we want to be installing. This can be accomplished with npm (starting with version 5) and its *package-lock.json* manifest, as well as through Facebook's Yarn package manager and its *yarn.lock* manifest, either of which we should be publishing to our versioned repository.

Using these manifests across environments ensures that we get reproducible installs of our dependencies. Everyone working with the codebase, as well as hosted environments, deal with the same package versions, both at the top level (direct dependencies) and regardless the nesting depth (dependencies of dependencies of dependencies).

Every dependency in our application should be explicitly declared in our manifest, relying on globally installed packages or global variables as little as possible—and ideally, not at all. Implicit dependencies involve additional steps across environments; developers and deployment flow alike must take action to ensure that these extra dependencies are installed, beyond what a simple `npm install` step could achieve. Here's an example of how a *package-lock.json* file might look:

```
{
  "name": "A",
  "version": "0.1.0",
  // metadata...
  "dependencies": {
    "B": {
      "version": "0.0.1",
      "resolved": "https://registry.npmjs.org/B/-/B-0.0.1.tgz",
      "integrity": "sha512-DeAdb33F+"
      "dependencies": {
        "C": {
          "version": "git://github.com/org/C.git#5c380ae3"
        }
      }
    }
  }
}
```

```
        }
    }
```

Using the information in a package lock file, which contains details about every package we depend upon and all of their dependencies as well, package managers can take steps to install the same bits every time, preserving our ability to quickly iterate and install package updates, while keeping our code safe.

Always installing identical versions of our dependencies—and identical versions of our dependencies' dependencies—brings us one step closer to having development environments that closely mirror what we do in production. This increases the likelihood that we can swiftly reproduce bugs that occurred in production in our local environments, while decreasing the odds that something that worked during development fails in staging.

6.3 Interfaces as Black Boxes

On a similar note to that of the preceding section, we should treat our own components no differently than how we treat third-party libraries and modules. Granted, we can make changes to our own code a lot more quickly than we can effect change in third-party code (if that's at all possible, in some cases). However, when we treat all components and interfaces (including our own HTTP API) as if they were foreign to us, we can focus on consuming and testing against interfaces, while ignoring the underlying implementation.

One way to improve our interfaces is to write detailed documentation about the input that an interface touchpoint expects, and how it affects the output it provides in each case. The process of writing documentation leads to uncovering limitations in the way the interface is designed, and we might decide to change it as a result. Consumers love good documentation because it means less fumbling about with the implementation (or its implementors) to understand how the interface is meant to be consumed, and whether it can accomplish what they need.

Avoiding distinctions helps us write unit tests where we mock dependencies that aren't under test, regardless of whether they were developed inhouse or by a third party. When writing tests, we always assume that third-party modules are generally well-tested enough that it's not our responsibility to include them in our test cases. The same thinking should apply to first-party modules that just happen to be dependencies of the module we're currently writing tests for.

This same reasoning can be applied to security concerns such as input sanitization. Regardless of the kind of application we're developing, we can't trust user input unless it's sanitized. Malicious actors could be angling to take over our servers or our customers' data, or otherwise inject content onto our web pages. These users might be customers or even employees, so we shouldn't treat them differently depending on that, when it comes to input sanitization.

Putting ourselves in the shoes of the consumer is the best tool to guard against half-baked interfaces. When—as a thought exercise— you stop and think about how you'd want to consume an interface, and the different ways in which you might need to consume it, you end up with a much better interface as a result. This is not to say we want to enable consumers to be able to do just about everything, but we want to make affordances so consuming an interface becomes as straightforward as possible and doesn't feel like a chore. If consumers are all but required to include long blocks of business logic right after they consume an interface, we need to stop ourselves and ask: would that business logic belong behind the interface rather than at its doorstep?

6.4 Build, Release, Run

Build processes have multiple aspects. At the highest level, the shared logic is where we install and compile our assets so that they can be consumed by our runtime application. This can mean installing system or application dependencies, copying files over to a different directory, compiling files into a different language, or bundling them together, among a multitude of other requirements your application might have.

Having clearly defined and delineated build processes is key when it comes to successfully managing an application across development, staging, and production environments. Each of these commonplace environments, and other environments you might encounter, is used for a specific purpose and benefits from being geared toward that purpose.

For development, we focus on enhanced debugging facilities, using development versions of libraries, source maps, and verbose logging levels. We also rely on custom ways of overriding behavior, so that we can easily mimic how the production environment would look. Where possible, we also throw in a real-time debugging server that takes care of restarting our application when code changes, applying CSS changes without refreshing the page, and so on.

In staging, we want an environment that closely resembles production, so we'll avoid most debugging features. But we might still want source maps and verbose logging to be able to trace bugs with ease. Our primary goal with staging environments generally is to weed out as many bugs as possible before the production push. Therefore, it is vital that these environments represent this middle ground between debugging affordance and production resemblance.

Production focuses more heavily on minification, optimizing images statically to reduce their byte size, and advanced techniques like route-based bundle splitting, where we serve only modules that are actually used by the pages visited by a user. We might rely on the tree shaking step, where we statically analyze our module graph and remove functions that aren't being used. Advanced techniques such as critical CSS inlining, where we precompute the most frequently used CSS styles so that we can inline them in the page and defer the rest of the styles to an asynchronous model that has a quicker time to interactive, can also be a boon. Security features, such as a hardened `Content-Security-Policy` policy that mitigates attack vectors like XSS or CSRF are often more stringent in production as well.

Testing also plays a significant role when it comes to processes around an application. Testing is typically done in two stages. Locally, developers test before a build, making sure linters don't produce any errors or that tests aren't failing. Then, before merging code into the mainline repository, we often run tests in a continuous integration (CI) environment to ensure that we don't merge broken code into our application. When it comes to CI, we start off by building our application, and then test against that, making sure the compiled application is in order.

For these processes to be effective, they must be consistent. Intermittent test failures feel worse than not having tests for the particular part of our application we're having trouble testing, because these failures affect every single test job. When tests fail in this way, we can no longer feel confident that a passing build means everything is in order, and this translates directly into decreased morale and increased frustration across the team as well. When an intermittent test failure is identified, the best course of action is to eliminate the intermittence as soon as possible, either by fixing the source of the intermittence, or by removing the test entirely. If the test is removed, make sure to file a ticket so that a well-functioning test is added later. Intermittence in test failures can be a symptom of bad design, and in our quest to fix these failures, we might resolve architecture issues along the way.

As we'll extensively discuss in the fourth book in the Modular JavaScript series, numerous services can aid with the CI process. Travis (*https://mjavascript.com/out/travis*) offers a quick way to get started integration testing your applications by connecting to your project's Git repository and running a command of your choosing; an exit code of 0 means the CI job passes, and a different exit code means the CI job failed. Codecov (*https://mjavascript.com/out/codecov*) can help out on the code coverage side, ensuring that most code paths in our application logic are covered by test cases. Solutions like WebPagetest (*https://mjavascript.com/out/wpt*), PageSpeed (*https://mjavascript.com/out/pagespeed*), and Lighthouse (*https://mjavascript.com/out/lighthouse*) can be integrated into the CI process we run on a platform like Travis to ensure that changes to our web applications don't have a negative impact on performance. Running these hooks on every commit and even in pull request branches can help keep bugs and regressions out of the mainline of your applications, and thus out of staging and production environments.

Note that until this point, we have focused on how we build and test our assets, but not on how we deploy them. These two processes, build and deployment, are closely related but shouldn't be intertwined. A clearly isolated build process that ends with a packaged application we can easily deploy, and a deployment process that takes care of the specifics regardless of whether you're deploying to your own local environment or to a hosted staging or production environment, means that, for the most part, we won't need to worry about environments during our build processes nor at runtime.

6.5 Statelessness

We've already explored how state, if left unchecked, can lead us straight to the heat death of our applications. Keeping state to a minimum translates directly into applications that are easier to debug.

The less global state there is, the less unpredictable the current conditions of an application are at any one point in time, and the fewer surprises we'll run into while debugging.

One particularly insidious form of state is caching. A cache is a great way to increase performance in an application by avoiding expensive lookups most of the time. When state management tools are used as a caching mechanism, we might fall into a trap; different bits and pieces of derived application state are derived at different points in time, thus rendering different bits of the application by using data computed at different points in time.

Derived state should seldom be treated as state that's separate from the data it was derived from. When it's not separate, we might run into situations where the original data is updated, but the derived state is not, so it becomes stale and inaccurate. When, instead, we always compute derived state from the original data, we reduce the likelihood that this derived state will become stale.

State is almost ubiquitous, and practically a synonym of applications, because applications without state aren't particularly useful. The question then arises: how can we better manage state? If we look at applications such as your typical web server, its main job is to receive requests, process them, and send back the appropriate responses. Consequently, web servers associate state to each request, keeping it near request handlers, the most relevant consumer of request state. There is as little global state as possible when it comes to web servers, with the vast majority of state contained in each request/response cycle instead. In this way, web servers save themselves a world of trouble when setting up horizontal scaling with multiple server nodes. In that way, they don't need to communicate with each other in order to maintain consistency across web server nodes. Ultimately, stateless servers refer to a data persistence layer, which is responsible for the application state, acting as the source of truth from which all other state is derived.

When a request results in a long-running job (such as sending out an email campaign, modifying records in a persistent database, etc.), it's best to hand that off into a separate service that, again, mostly keeps state regarding that job. Separating services into specific needs means we can keep web servers lean and stateless, and improve our flows by adding more servers, persistent queues (so that we don't drop jobs), and so on. When every task is tethered together through tight coupling and state, it could become challenging to maintain, upgrade, and scale a service over time.

Derived state in the form of caches is common in the world of web servers. In the case of a personal website with books available for download, for instance, we might be tempted to store the PDF representation of each book in a file, so that we don't have to recompile the PDF whenever the corresponding */book* route is visited. When the book is updated, we'd recompute the PDF file and flush it to disk again, so that this derived state remains fresh. When our web server ceases to be single-node and we start using a cluster of several nodes, however, it might not be so trivial to broadcast the news about books being updated across nodes, and thus it'd be best to leave derived state to the persistence layer. Otherwise, a web server node might receive the request to update a book, perform the update, and recompute the PDF file on that node, but we'd be failing to invalidate the PDF files being served by other nodes, which would have and continue to serve stale copies of the PDF representation.

A better alternative in such a case is to store derived state in a data store like Redis or Amazon S3, either of which we could update from any web server, and then serve precomputed results from Redis directly. In this way, we'd still be able to access the latency benefits of using precomputed derived state, but at the same time we'd stay resilient when these requests or updates can happen on multiple web server nodes.

On Disposability

Whenever we hook up an event listener, regardless of whether we're listening for DOM events or those from an event emitter, we should also strongly consider disposing of the listener when the concerned parties are no longer interested in the event being raised. For instance, if we have a React component that, upon mount, starts listening for `resize` events on the `window` object, we should also make sure we remove those event listeners when the component is unmounted.

This kind of diligence ensures that we can set up and tear down bits of our application without leaving behind mounting piles of listeners that would result in memory leaks, which are hard to track down and pinpoint.

The concept of disposability goes beyond just event handlers, though. Any sort of resource that we allocate and attach to an object, component, or service, should be released and cleaned up when that attachment ceases to exist. This way, we can confidently create and dispose of as many components as we want, without putting our application's performance at risk.

Another improvement that could aid in complexity management is to structure applications so that all business logic is contained in a single directory structure (for example, *lib/* or *services/*) acting as a physical layer where we keep all the logic together. In doing so, we'll open ourselves up for more opportunities to reuse logic, because team members will know to go looking here before reimplementing slightly different functions that perform more or less similar computations for derived state.

Colocation of view components with its immediate counterparts is appealing—that is, keeping each view's main component, child components, controllers, and logic in the same structure. However, doing so in a way that tightly couples business logic to specific components can be detrimental to having a clear understanding of the way an application works as a whole.

Large client-side applications often suffer from not having a single place where logic should be deposited. As a result, the logic is instead spread among components, view controllers, and the API, instead of being mostly handled in the server side, and then in a single physical location in the client-side code structure. This centralization can be key for newcomers to the team seeking to better understand the way the application flows, because otherwise they'd have to go fishing around our view components and controllers in order to ascertain what's going on. This is a daunting proposition when first dipping our toes in the uncharted shores of a new codebase.

The same case could be made about any other function of our code, as having clearly defined layers in an application can make it straightforward to understand the way an algorithm flows from layer to layer. But we'll find the biggest rewards to reap when it comes to isolating business logic from the rest of the application code.

Using a state management solution like Redux or MobX, where we isolate all state from the rest of the application, is another option. Regardless of our approach, the most important aspect remains that we stick to clearly isolating the view-rendering aspects in our applications from the business logic aspects as much as possible.

6.6 Parity in Development and Production

We've established the importance of having clearly defined build and deployment processes. In a similar vein, we have the different application environments including development, production, staging, feature branches, SaaS versus on-premises environments, and so on. Environments are divergent by definition. We are going to end up with different features in different environments, whether they are debugging facilities, product features, or performance optimizations.

Whenever we incorporate environment-specific feature flags or logic, we need to pay attention to the discrepancies introduced by these changes. Could the environment-dependent logic be tightened so that the bare-minimum divergence is introduced? Should we isolate the newly introduced logic fork into a single module that takes care of as many aspects of the divergence as possible? Could the flags that are enabled as we're developing features for a specific environment result in inadvertently introducing bugs into other environments where a different set of flags is enabled?

Conversely, the opposite is true. As with many things programming, creating these divergences is relatively easy, whereas deleting them might prove most challenging. This difficulty arises from the unknown situations that we might not typically run into during development or unit testing, but that are still valid situations in our production environments.

As an example, consider the following scenario. We have a production application using `Content-Security-Policy` rules to mitigate malicious attack vectors. For the development environment, we also add a few extra rules like `'unsafe-inline'`, which lets our developer tools manipulate the page so that code and style changes are reloaded without requiring a full page refresh, speeding up our precious development productivity and saving time. Our application already has a component that users can leverage to edit programming source code, but we now have a requirement to change that component.

We swap the current component with a new one from our company's own component framework, so we know it's battle-tested and works well in other production applications developed in house. We test things in our local development environment, and everything works as expected. Tests pass. Other developers review our code, test locally in their own environments as well, and find nothing wrong with it. We merge our code, and a couple of weeks later deploy to production. Before long, we start getting support requests about the code-editing feature being broken, and need to roll back the changeset that introduced the new code editor.

What went wrong? We didn't notice that the new component doesn't work unless `style-src: 'unsafe-inline'` is present. Given that we allow inline styles in development, catering to our convenient developer tools, this wasn't a problem during development or local testing performed by our teammates. However, when we deploy to production, which follows a stricter set of CSP rules, the `'unsafe-inline'` rule is not served, and the component breaks down.

The problem here is that we had a divergence in parity that prevented us from identifying a limitation in the new component: it uses inline styles to position the text cursor. This is at odds with our strict CSP rules, but it can't be properly identified because our development environment is more lax about CSP than production is.

As much as possible, we should strive to keep these kinds of divergences to a minimum. If we don't, bugs might find their way to production, and a customer might end up reporting the bug to us. Merely being aware of discrepancies like this is not enough. It's not practical nor effective to keep these logic gates in your head so that whenever you're implementing a change, you mentally go through the motions of how the change would differ if your code was running in production instead.

Proper integration testing might catch many of these kinds of mistakes, but that won't always be the case.

6.7 Abstraction Matters

Eager abstraction can result in catastrophe. Conversely, failure to identify and abstract away sources of major complexity can be incredibly costly as well. When we consume complex interfaces directly, but don't necessarily take advantage of all the advanced configuration options that an interface has to offer, we are missing out on a powerful abstraction we could be using. The alternative is to create a middle layer in front of the complex interface, and have consumers go through that layer instead.

This intermediate layer would be in charge of calling the complex abstraction itself, but offers a simpler interface with fewer configuration options and improved ease of use for the use cases that matter to us. Often, complicated or legacy interfaces demand that we offer up data that could be derived from other parameters being passed into the function call. For example, we might be asked how many adults, how many children, and how many people in total are looking to make a flight booking, even though the latter can be derived from the former. Other examples include expecting fields to be in a particular string format (such as a date string that could be derived from a native JavaScript date instead), using nomenclature that's relevant to the implementation but not so much to the consumer, or a lack of sensible defaults (required fields that are rarely changed into anything other than a recommended value that isn't set by default).

When we're building out a web application that consumes a highly parametized API in order to search for the cheapest hassle-free flights, for example, and we anticipate consuming this API in a few different ways, it would cost us dearly not to abstract away most of the parameters demanded by the API that do not fit our use case. This middle layer can take care of establishing sensible default values and of converting reasonable data structures such as native JavaScript dates or case-insensitive airport codes into the formats demanded by the API we're using.

In addition, our abstraction could also take care of any follow-up API calls that need to be made in order to hydrate data. For example, a flight search API might return an airline code for each different flight, such as AA for American Airlines, but a UI consumer would also necessitate to hydrate AA into a display name for the airline, accompanied by a logo to embed on the user interface, and perhaps even a quick link to its check-in page.

When we call into the backing API every time, with the full query, appeasing its quirks and shortcomings instead of taking the abstracted approach, it will not only be difficult to maintain an application that consumes those endpoints in more than one place, but also becomes a challenge down the road, when we want to include results from a different provider (which of course will have its own set of quirks and shortcomings). At this point, we would have two separate sets of API calls, one for each provider, and each massaging the data to accommodate provider-specific quirks in a module that shouldn't be concerned with such matters, but only the results themselves.

A middle layer could leverage a normalized query from the consumer, such as the one where we took a native date and then formatted it when calling the flight search API, and then adapt that query into either of the backing services that actually produce flight search results. This way, the consumer has to deal with only a single, simplified interface, while having the ability to seamlessly interact with two similar backing services that offer different interfaces.

The same case could, and should, be made for the data structures returned from either of these backing services. By normalizing the data into a structure that contains only information that's relevant to our consumers, and augmenting it with the derived information they need (such as the airline name and details as explained earlier), consumers can focus on their own concerns while leveraging a data structure that's close to their needs. At the same time, this normalization empowers our abstraction to merge results from both backing services and treat them as if they came from a single source: the abstraction itself, leaving the backing services as mere implementation details.

When we rely directly on the original responses, we may find ourselves writing view components that are more verbose than they need to be. These components contain logic to pull together the different bits of metadata needed to render our views, map data from the API representation into what we actually want to display, and then map user input back into what the API expects. With a layer in between, we can keep this mapping logic contained in a single place, and leave the rest of our application unencumbered by it.

Mastering modular JavaScript isn't strictly about following a well-defined set of rules, but rather about being able to put yourself in the shoes of your consumers by planning for feature development that may be coming down the pipe (but not too extensively) and treating documentation with the same respect and care that you should be putting into interface design. The internals, as the implementation details that they are, can always be improved later. Of course, we'll want to patch—or at least abstract away—those sources of complexity, but it is in their shell that beautiful modules truly shine. Above all, trust your own judgment and don't let the latest development fads clog your decision making!

Index

immutability, 91
incidental state, 88-90
inheritance, 109-110, 113
input sanitization, 131
interfaces
    as black boxes, 130-131
    complexity hidden by, 1-3
    documenting, 59-60
    resiliency in, 33-37
    simplicity in, 38-39
    tiny surface area of, 39
    touchpoints of, 2, 25-27, 48
    well-designed, benefits of, 10,
        23-25, 55
iterators, 106

J

JavaScript
    books about, viii
    history of modularity in, 3-10,
        13-15
    modern features of, 99-108
    modular design with (see modular
        design)
JSON, 119-121

L

layers
    for business logic, 2, 136
    for horizontal scaling, 11
    when needed, 52, 69

M

maintainability, 10
message passing, 119-121
MobX, 137
modular design, 1-3
    (see also development methodol-
        ogy)
    abstractions in (see abstractions)
    benefits of, 10-11
    books about, viii
    composition in (see composition)
    CRUST principles for, 31-39
    granularity with, 2, 11-13
    interfaces in (see interfaces)
    JavaScript features for, 99-108

JavaScript history of, 3-10, 13-15
    necessity of, 13-15
    patterns for (see patterns)
    readability in, 36
    scalability with (see scalability)
    SRP (single responsibility princi-
        ple), 19-23
    state management in, 29-31
module-level design
    composability, 42-45
    context of, considering, 62
    CRUST principles for, 50-56
    data structures in, 92-97
    debugging, 58
    documentation, 59-61
    error handling, 57
    frameworks for, 68-69
    nesting, reducing complexity of,
        66-67
    pace of development, 46-50
    priorities for, 55-56
    refactoring code (see refactoring
        code)
    removing code, 61-62
    requirements of, limiting, 45-46
    scalability, 42-45
    splitting modules, 51-55
    state, minimizing, 86-92
    testing, 58
    tight coupling, avoiding, 67
"Move Fast and Break Things" man-
    tra, 49
multiline strings, 99

N

nconf npm package, 125
nesting, reducing complexity of,
    66-67, 79-81
Node.js, 7
NODE_ENV variable, 125

O

object factories, 30, 115-119
object spread, 104
online resources, for this book, xi

P

parity divergences, minimizing, 137-138
patterns
    callback hell, 66, 79-81
    event emission, 119
    IIFE, 4
    message passing, 119-121
    object factories, 30, 115-119
    promise hell, 66, 81
    revealing module, 25-27, 114-115
performance
    priority of, 13, 56, 90
    Webpack features for, 9
persistence, 88, 134
    (see also state)
production build processes, 132
promise hell pattern, 66, 81
promises, 106-108
pure functions, 29, 92
pyramidal code structure, 74-76

R

React, 14
readability, 36, 51, 70-72
README-driven development, 60
realized state, 88
Redis, 135
Redux, 137
refactoring
    branch flipping, 72-74
    breaking apart functions, 84-86
    determining when needed, 65, 70
    extracting functions, 76-79
    guard clauses, 72-74
    nested callbacks, flattening, 79
    pyramidal structure for, 74-76
    for similar tasks, 82-84
    variables used in, 70-72
RequireJS, 5-7
resiliency, 33-37
rest parameters, 102-104
reusability
    code removal and, 62
    functions for, 82-84
revealing module pattern, 25-27, 114-115

S

scalability
    horizontal, with composition, 42-45, 109
    horizontal, with layers, 11, 69
    vertical, with inheritance, 109
scope
    global scope, 4, 10
    hoisting and, 74
    nesting and, 67-68, 79
    removing functions from, 77
<script> tag, 3
security
    configuration management, 123-128
    input sanitization, 131
    in production, 132, 137
shapes
    consistent, benefits of, 3, 32, 37
    consistent, finding, 82
    data structures determining, 93
short circuits (see guard clauses)
simplicity, 38-39, 55
spread operator, 104
SRP (single responsibility principle), 10, 19-23
staging build processes, 132
state
    caching, 134-135
    complexity of, 29, 86-88
    containing, 90-91
    as entropy, 29, 86
    ephemeral, 88
    incidental, 88-90
    levels of, 29
    minimizing, 29-31, 86-92, 133-137
    realized, 88
state management solution, 137
stateless servers, 134
strings, template literals for, 99
surface area, tiny, 39

T

TDD (test-driven design), 60
template literals, 99
testing, 58, 132
tight coupling, 67

tiny surface areas, 39
touchpoints, exposing, 2, 25-27, 48
Twelve Factor App, 123

U
unambiguity, 37
underscore "_" prefix, 25-27

V
variables, readability increased by, 70-72

W
Webpack, 9
website resources, for this book, xi

About the Author

Nicolás Bevacqua is a senior software engineer at Elastic. He is the author of several JavaScript books, including *JavaScript Application Design* (Manning, 2015), *Practical Modern JavaScript* (O'Reilly, 2017), and *Mastering Modular JavaScript* (O'Reilly, 2018), as well as the editor of *ponyfoo.com*. Nicolás has experience not only in working on JavaScript problems, but also in sharing his applied learning with others. You can find him on Twitter as @nzgb.

Colophon

The cover fonts are Helvetica Inserat and DIN. The text font is Adobe Minion Pro; the heading font is Adobe Myriad Condensed; and the code font is Dalton Maag's Ubuntu Mono.

Learn from experts.
Find the answers you need.

Sign up for a **10-day free trial** to get **unlimited access** to all of the content on Safari, including Learning Paths, interactive tutorials, and curated playlists that draw from thousands of ebooks and training videos on a wide range of topics, including data, design, DevOps, management, business—and much more.

Start your free trial at:
oreilly.com/safari

(No credit card required)